OIKOYMENH

KAROLINUM PRESS

EDICE OIKÚMENÉ

Svazek 141

JAN PATOČKA

Living in Problematicity

*Edited and translated
by Eric Manton*

PRAGUE
2020

Filosofický ústav AV ČR, v. v. i.
www.flu.cas.cz

OIKOYMENH
www.oikoymenh.cz

Karolinum Press
www.karolinum.cz

Cataloguing-in-Publication Data is available
from the National Library of the Czech Republic

To Patočka's Students:

Remember and reclaim your role as dissidents,
for it is the authentic philosophical manner
of caring for one's soul.
It is not only your calling,
but also your responsibility.

Table of Contents

Editor's Preface

This present booklet is the introductory installment of what is intended to be a comprehensive examination of that which is political in the life and thought of Jan Patočka.

This interest arose from my search for the answer to the question of dissidence: why do the few rise up when the many do not; what is peculiar about those people who stood up for their beliefs that differed from the majority which just goes along or offers little if any resistance to injustice and authoritarian tendencies. I became interested in this question after reflecting on the transformations of 1989 in Europe. I had hoped that something could be learned from their example that could support other people that are still struggling and resisting oppression of various kinds.

I chose to focus my search on the Czech dissidents under Communism, because they engaged in philosophical reflection on the nature and circumstances of dissidence, i.e., reflection on what it is and why one must become a dissident when faced with injustice. The writings of Václav Havel, members of Charter 77, and other dissidents showed the depth of this philosophical approach to examining the role of the responsible person under totalitarianism. This level of philosophical reflection was rarely seen in other countries of the Soviet bloc. While I looked for examples in other countries as well, I found the most valuable sources here in Prague.

During my quest, it was very often repeated to me that if I wanted to understand the philosophy of the dissidents, then I would first have to understand the philosophical thought of Jan Patočka. Almost everyone I talked to was either a student of Patočka, a student of one of his students, or had read many of his works and was inspired not only by his activity with Charter 77, but especially by the message his philosophy gave to them.

Before I was able to read Patočka's writings in the original Czech, I read Erazim Kohák's *Jan Patočka: Philosophy and Selected Wri-*

tings, published a few years earlier in 1989, which was extremely useful. When my knowledge of Czech improved, the staff of the Archive of Jan Patočka taught me not only the language, but helped me understand the philosophy as well.

My attempts to discover clues to a philosophy of political dissidence in Patočka's works, i.e., some sort of political philosophy of Jan Patočka, often met with skepticism and I was advised to try something else. Patočka is known as a phenomenologist (a mediator between Husserl and Heidegger), a philosopher of history, and a historian of philosophy—but with a political philosophy? Unlikely. While still today "that which is political" in his thought is not very well known, his ideas about the political world and our proper engagement with it are receiving more attention. Here I must thank Martin Palouš for being one of the few that agreed with me in those early days.

My original intention was to put together a book that would be a comprehensive presentation of Patočka's political philosophy. This book would contain translations of the key works that have not yet been translated and an extensive commentary drawn from the Master's thesis I wrote at Charles University on "The Political Philosophy of Jan Patočka". My subsequent decision to return to the political sphere and engage in human rights work delayed this project.

However, with the occasion of the memorial conference honoring the 100 years since his birth and 30 years since his death, it became apparent that the time had come to share at least part of this project—hence this present booklet.

I hope that this first installment will be considered a manifestation of my gratitude to all of my friends in Prague that not only taught me about Patočka, but also about so much more—that is an immense debt that can never truly be repaid.

Therefore, I wish to acknowledge and thank the many people and institutions that have supported me over the years in my research on Czech dissident political philosophy and on Jan Patočka specifically. My sincere appreciation and grateful thanks go to:

Aleš Havlíček, who first suggested I continue my research and get a degree at Charles University. Thanks to him also for publishing this booklet.

Ivan Havel and the Center for Theoretical Study for adopting me those many years ago and teaching me more than they will ever know.

Laďka Švandová and everyone at the Jan Patočka Archive in Prague for their years of patience, guidance, and support.

The Research Support Scheme of the Central European University for their support for the writing of my thesis.

Klaus Nellen of the Institut für die Wissenschaften vom Menschen in Vienna for his support and encouragement and who was deservedly recognized for all his hard work with the Patočka Archive in Vienna by being awarded a Patočka medal.

Ludger Hagedorn for consistently being my most honest and most constructive critic and partner. These translations could not have been realized without him.

Erazim Kohák for facilitating my discovery of Patočka's philosophy with his seminal book, and for his translating of Extramundane.

Robin Cassling for advising on the linguistic formulations in this booklet.

Ida for all her love and support, and her patience and tolerance.

And special thanks to the Director of the Jan Patočka Archive in Prague, Co-Director of CTS, repeated visiting fellow of IWM, my mentor and very good friend, Ivan Chvatík, who helped me figure out the complicated philosophical formulations in these texts. He is a wonderful example of someone who is living in problematicity.

Eric Manton
Praha, April 2007

Platonism and Politics

(1933)

In the most recent issue of *Česká mysl* (Czech Thought), Dr. Smetáček polemically opposed political Platonism, reproached it for its inconsistency, but moreover, for some kind of principal inability to assert itself realistically in life.[1] Smetáček does not principally prove this point, but instead just analyzes Benda's "Discours à la nation européenne".[2] Presently Benda only interests me secondarily. What is more important for me is the principal question concerning Platonism and Plato, and whether Benda, if he truly does make a mistake, makes it as a Platonic. The root of the whole question, in my opinion, is that Plato is the person who conceived of a society which is governed purely spiritually and founded on the life of the spirit, which according to Plato – and I do not consider his view once and for all discounted – has its own special organ in philosophy as Plato conceives it, that is, in a science of absolute rationale that is concerned with being itself and with the ultimate bases of all value. The ultimate meaning of Platonism is, I think, a spiritual *universum*, which a person penetrates by means of a certain purely inner and active (but definitely not mythical) purification. This purification or philosophy is at the same time the most important and most intensive *praxis*, solely able to give a necessary unity to the life of the individual and of society, to give to life that inner center that one potentially nurses within oneself as the unfulfilled meaning of one's life. Thus, Plato's political conception means, in brief, this: 1) there exists a single and coherent, truly human, spiritual behavior called philosophy; 2) the "object" of philosophy is not primarily the contents

---

[1] Z. Smetáček, "Platonism a politika", in: *Česká mysl* XXIX, (1933), pp. 109–113. *Ed.*

[2] J. Benda, "Discours à la nation européenne", in: *La Nouvelle Revue Française*, 1933. *Ed.*

of this world; 3) the right of philosophy to establish norms for life consists in its inner truthfulness, in its absolute character; 4) all of human activity, not founded on philosophy and not illuminated throughout by philosophy, has the character of dissatisfaction, false-hood, and a lack of inner order. As a supporting argument to this, a parenthetical note: Plato is not an "intellectual" in a kind of modified modern conception, a person who only states things and accumulates information and skills. Greek philosophy (even for Aristotle) has abso-lutely nothing in common with anything like this, and it is not possible in Greek philosophy to interpret a dualism of "theory and *praxis*", as Greek philosophy went through that and parted ways with right at its start. Certainly, men like Heraclites and Empedocles did not philoso-phize for entertainment, nor were they "armchair philosophers". The Greek words νοεῖν and νόησις and even φρόνησις and ἐπιστήμη mean something quite different than our words "thinking" or "mere observing", etc., which do not affect us, which are merely "taken into account".

Thus the question is posed: is Platonism, conceived thus, once and for all discounted, or does it exist in a certain modified form even in our own lives? This is the question of Benda's treason of the intellec-tuals.[3] Benda overestimated modern intellectualism and its philoso-phical worth; not every intellectualism means a step down the path of spiritualism, although historically intellectualism comes from a weak-ening of and splitting from spiritualism. Intellectualism as mere in-quisitiveness, as a mode of mundane life, as a way to fill time, or a mode of aestheticism, is no closer to the "spiritual" life of the plato-nic ideal than the technicism, mysticism, and particularism proscribed by Benda. Just like these, intellectualism is, in its centrifugal tendency, a mere mask of the spirit, a comfortable and simple mask. Platonism can only live where those vital hypotheses discussed above on which Platonism is built also exist. But then the meaning of Platonism is identical to the meaning of true philosophizing in general. The philo-sopher, in the true sense of the word, can see the practical unrealizabi-lity of the platonic ideal in a given moment or even in general; as a philosopher, however, he cannot not innerly acknowledge the plato-nic ideal and be its adherent. For the real philosopher, i.e., who metho-

---

[3] J. Benda, *La Trahison des clercs*, 1927. *Ed.*

dically and thematically awakens within himself the hidden meaning of humanity, there is no other possible path. The philosopher as such is undoubtedly not engaged in daily political conflict, in daily *praxis*, which is always based on sophistry or mysticism, but his activity in the world is based on the philosopher possessing a political idea, on the philosopher living within Plato's political idea. One of today's preeminent philosophers described the function of philosophy as such: *ein universales und letztrationales Selbstbewußtsein der Menschheit zu schaffen, durch welches sie auf die Bahn echter Menschheit gebracht werden soll.*[4] And the impact of philosophy in life is not fascination, as Benda thinks, but rather it is the permeation, gradually and usually distortedly, of philosophical concepts into the common human consciousness. If philosophy and Man essentially belong together, then the platonic political idea is something unfading. Then, of course, there is no remedy to the "treason of the intellectuals" by the practicing of intellectualism, by the turn from *praxis* to "theory" etc., but rather the only remedy is philosophy. And philosophy does not appear on command, but rather it is, as Plato perceived well in *The Republic*, a matter of enormous grace "a calling, which is possible to properly perform only if its adept is endowed with memory, astuteness of the spirit, and a noble and affable mind; if its adept is a friend and ally of truth, justice, strength and temperance".[5] Moreover, the philosopher has a long, difficult, and steadfast pedagogical task, which is essentially never finished. The tension of the political idea of philosophy consists in the fact that philosophy is a matter of the few.

A tension that certainly is one of the themes of Plato's philosophical thought. And Plato is the first to see – and this is truly what Benda borrowed from Plato – the moderating and mediating moment in myth.

---

[4] "to create a universal and ultimately rational self-consciousness of humankind, by which humankind will be brought onto the path of true humanity", E. Husserl, *Die Idee einer philosophischen Kultur. Japanisch-deutsche Zeitschrift für Wissenschaft und Technik,* Bd. I, Heft 2, Lübeck 1923. *Ed.*

[5] Plato, *The Republic*, Book VI, 487a. This is the editor's translation from the Czech, which has been left in because it sounds more appropriate than the Bloom translation, for example, which is as follows: "a practice like this that a man could never adequately pursue if he were not by nature a rememberer, a good learner, magnificent, charming, and a friend and kinsman of truth, justice, courage, and moderation…" *Ed.*

Myth, for Plato, is usually a symbol in place of higher understanding, a symbol that suggests unity and continuity, and is the expression of this unity and continuity. Myth is, at least in most cases, an imaginative vestment of truth; that is why it is useful for life realized on a lower level to move within myth. It can be difficult to live in philosophy because philosophy is the unceasing struggle against the natural direction of life, but those who cannot or do not want to live in philosophy can live in a proper myth. This proper myth is necessary because myth is a special form of the collective spirit of a certain level, and if there will not be proper myths, there will be improper ones. In this spirit, Plato proposes his philosophical myth as a philosophical formation of the naive manifestation of spiritual needs, which express themselves in an instinct for mythology, i.e., the myth in the third book of *The Republic* concerning the four elements that humankind is composed of and on which the platonic caste system should be based.[6]

If the foundations which today's political movements and political systems are based upon were researched, it would be seen that they are myths which admittedly have, here and there, a relation to truly philosophical motives, but on the whole they are of an anti-spiritual nature. The most spiritual myth, Christianity, is, on the whole, on the retreat. Its lay derivation, humanism, is ever more intellectual, pallid, and ineffectual, without *pathos*. Collectivism has nowhere yet overcome its distrust of spirituality, which refuses to abide by collectivism's norms. If we accept the platonic view of the necessary dualism of philosophy and myth, then Benda is correct in calling for a new myth. It is just that this myth cannot be a poorly created intellectual fantasy, or a cumbersomely fabricated program of instruction, but rather a real, living manifestation of poetical, philosophical yearning. It cannot be a manifestation of feebleness or laziness, nor can there be a ruse in this myth. It is only possible to build such a myth on a great philosophy. Benda does not have nor know philosophy like this; he stays, on the whole, in line with the Enlightenment. Today, however, what is important is a new Enlightenment, one that would not lead to a superficial, mundane rationality caused by emphasizing the human principle against the divine, against which the fight seems to be finished.

---

6   Plato, *The Republic*, Book III, 414d–415c. *Ed.*

These lines do not have any other purpose than to bring attention to a certain aspect of how Platonism relates to myth. Benda's philosophy of history does not quite get it right. Also, Benda's concept of myth and the different aspects of the life of the soul do not, from a purely platonic point of view, seem to me to be correct.

Some Comments Concerning
the Extramundane and Mundane Position
of Philosophy

(1934)

These few comments lay no claim to being themselves philosophy. They do not deal with philosophical problems proper, nor do they pretend to be a contribution to the philosophical dialogue between the ages, often occurring over millennia; a dialogue of those whose very existence in time negates time even more than that of the poet and the hero, a dialogue measured in eternity. All greatness consists ultimately in the extratemporal penetrating into time; philosophical greatness is, moreover, an explicit comprehension of the unity of the temporal and the supratemporal. Yet is not our time, to which the greatness of the poet and the hero is so alien, even more estranged from the greatness of philosophy? Is it not part of the concept of such a philosopher that he sees his whole life solely as material for philosophizing, so that he is not a philosopher only now and then, that philosophy is not for him only one among his many other petty vices and virtues, but his very being? By contrast, is not philosophy today something in life which we can simply take or leave? How can such a second-hand philosophy, devoid of passion, resist the onslaughts of "the world"? Is it not important that philosophy should, first and foremost, grasp what it is in its idea, and thus what it can be for a particular philosopher? There is something like the experience of philosophy, a demanding process to which no individual can lay claim himself, but which is, rather, the creation of the succession of the great. Several aspects I consider important about this experience constitute the theme of my improvisations. Let me repeat, this is not philosophy that I am doing here. It is only a modest attempt to rend philosophy from forgetting, it is an is an ἀνάμνησις an attempt, an attempt fully conscious of the risks it runs, like speaking of a third dimension in a two-dimensional world. In speaking briefly, I cannot justify my theses as I would wish, yet they are justified more deeply than the aphilosophical vacuity of some productions that shamelessly claim for themselves the name of philosophy.

Let us set out with the thesis that philosophy is the concrete carrying out of this general idea: 1) Among Man's possibilities there is the capacity for coming to know *the world* (not as particulars, but as "a whole"). 2) The subject can grasp this possibility only by, in some sense, leaving behind, transcending the world. 3) This knowledge is not random like the knowledge of particulars, and while never ever finished, it is *of a different order* than the intramundane understanding of particulars. 4) Only coming to know the world (as "a whole") provides the necessary unity for coming to know the world's contents, i.e., particulars.

To elaborate on these thoughts more deeply would mean to do philosophy and that is not our intention here. Let us now pose a question: if the philosopher is separated by a chasm from the world and so also from everything human (Man, after all, belongs among the "contents of the world"), then is not what he does irrelevant to us? Is not then the yardstick he applies to this world of ours nothing to us—and conversely, measured by our own standards might we not consider his profession only an intellectual game, fleeing the seriousness of life? Is it not one of the numerous distractions that humans can afford in times and places of well-being, in certain enclaves amid the world's storm? Does not, then, every honest working-man, everyone who suffers through life and who bears life's burden with at least a trace of strength and pride, have every right to look down upon such derelict like upon someone who basically does not know and is incapable of knowing what life is; and consequently, insofar as he nonetheless persists in trying to explain life in his own way, to look at him like at a counterfeiter of the meaning of life? Are not those right who see, behind the superhuman facade of the philosophic *profession de foi*, an all too human flight out of a fear of the truth of reality, be the reasons social or individual? Is not a philosopher destined, in his flight, to deceive himself and others? Is he not a pitiful clown, unintentionally comic because he is most dependent where he thinks himself free and because where he thinks himself wholly on his own he is most strongly determined by the drama of the human community? The world is neither indifferent nor defenseless before the philosopher. While the philosopher draws back from the world, the world for its part turns to him with *hatred*. From the standpoint of "the world", philosophy is a perversion and a trick, a tricky perversion. It can be tolerated, it can be put to use so that it does not become a burden, and it is advisable to do that when there is still time. If, though, philosophy will not want to serve, then it must be routed like an incomprehensible cancer gnawing on the life of the whole. It must be excised *utterly* out of all of life's functions and so deprived of its vitality. Of course, such objections *intrinsically* bypass philosophy itself, striking only the way it is perceived and expressed, in other words, the worldly projection of philosophy. All such objections are in vain already because they can never find philosophy itself, even if they traverse all that is, the entire universe—that is not where philosophy is. For us, people in the world, philosophy is a specter that goes "boo!" behind our backs, but can never be induced to confront us face to face. The hostile attitude to philosophy starts with the indifference towards philosophy, is intensified by the deepening of the separateness of philosophy which Heraclitus first mentioned and of which Meister Eckhart later spoke such marvelous words, and leads to the perception of philosophy as a danger, as a threat, and thence, to the hatred of philosophy.

Let us elaborate upon this more concretely, seeing the relation between philosophy and the world in its various aspects. The world is only able to see the mundane projection of philosophy; philosophy, however, sees the world as it really is—for that is its theme. The philosopher is externally defenseless before the world, and the world is internally defenseless before philosophy. That means that between the philosopher and the world there can really be no discussion about *philosophy*. The theses in terms of which the world interprets philosophy – all those materialisms, positivisms, economisms, psychologisms, psychiatrisms, sociologisms, theologisms – rest on the false assumption that a discussion with philosophy is possible on the level of this world. That is a position the philosopher cannot accept – if he did, he would be saying that it would at least be possible for philosophy to depend on some intramundane fact – and with that he would put an end to philosophy as the understanding of the whole.

Something else is linked with this. A philosopher can never convince others of his truth with proofs. Those who a priori conceive of the philosopher in such a way that they are incapable of understanding him, find in philosophical arguments only further proof of what they already believe. Proofs are possible only within a shared matrix of principles, and that is out of the question here: the argumentation against the philosopher is presented on the level of intramundane facts, and not on his own level. Hence, too, the philosopher's hesitation when asked to state what philosophy is: "For it does not at all admit of verbal expression".[1] How can there be a proof of something for which there is nothing analogous *within the world* and that, in a worldly projection, becomes but another part of the universal relativity of all things human? Thus *silence* becomes the manner of the philosophic answer.

As a philosopher cannot convince with proofs, so we can say in an even broader sense that his speech can never be understood. While using, for essential reasons, the same language as others, he endows words with a meaning they have not had before. In no thing does he see what those who do not reflect see in their naiveté. The words "world," "thing," "man" mean something essentially different for the philosopher than for us non-philosophers who have arrived at their meaning God knows how. Therefore, everything in philosophy seems stood on its head (Hegel said that *"Philosophie ist die verkehrte Welt"*),[2] the "real" becomes "unreal" and vice versa, things are determined by ideas rather than ideas by things. Karl Marx, opposing his naive (no pejorative connotations intended) mode of thought to Hegel's philosophy of right, observed that "Der Unterschied ruht nicht im Inhalt, sondern in der Betrachtungsweise oder in *der Sprachweise*".[3] The entire ambiguity of the relation between philosophy and the world appears in these words. The philosopher can accept every word here, but the meaning he will assign to them will contain a different idea than the one Karl Marx sought to express. Words that were to be a radical condemnation of philosophy as verbalism are implicitly a defeat for the world. Thus the philosopher is ironic in principle, even when he lets the world speak for him in speaking against him.

---

[1] Plato, *Seventh Letter*, 341c. *Ed.*

[2] "philosophy is the world inverted". *Ed.*

[3] "The difference lies not in the content but in the mode of thought or speaking." K. Marx, *Zur Kritik der Hegelschen Rechtsphilosophie*, in: K. Marx – F. Engels, *Werke, Gesamtausgabe (MEGA)*, Vol. I/2, Berlin 1982, p. 8 (line 32–33). *Ed.*

The putative history of philosophy is not simply a matter of tracing the life of philosophy itself as much as of the unremitting conflict between philosophy and the world. Philosophy discovered the world and went on to derive from it consequences for human life. Yet much of what is covered in textbooks under the title "Philosophy" is nothing more than the world's response to philosophy's call for a radical clarity and for the daring of thought. The first man who reflected explicitly on what philosophy is already had before him the phenomena of ostentatious erudition and sophistication, concealing its nature, and stigmatized them as such.[4] It was the same man who said of the principle of philosophy that it is incomprehensible for people both before and after they have heard of it.[5]

Heraclitus, to be sure, did not yet face the organized effort, assisted by science and religion, to be rid of philosophy that we face today. Science replaces the idea of knowing "*the whole*" with the idea of knowing *all there is*, all existing entities and relations; replacing the idea of knowing the world with the idea of knowing the world's contents; the idea of knowing the essence of things with the idea of a formal system of thought about things; the idea of understanding with the idea of research, which is ignorant of the contradiction between design and details, between conception and technique. Religion, in place of a transition from the level of existents to somewhere else, posits a primordial, irreducible and incomprehensible difference between two ontic levels; it posits the transcendent in place of transcendence.

Religion is indebted to philosophy at least in its conceptual structure, science in its origins. Yet precisely because what satisfies the ideal of science cannot satisfy the ideal of philosophy, the latter cannot be simply the "foundation of the sciences," as the neokantians conceived of it, a reflection about science in its actual existence. Since it cannot be a handmaiden where it should be the mistress, it cannot become the servant of the transcendent. Science and religion, divorced from philosophy, turn against it, becoming instruments of the violation of Man by mimetic substitute for the quest for truth. Science, grounded

---

[4] "Much learning will not teach wisdom, or it would have taught Hesiod and Pythagoras as well as Xenophanes and Heccaistos. For only one thing is wise: to know the idea that governs all throughout" (Heraclitus, Fr. B 40.). *Ed.*

[5] Heraclitus, Fr. B 1. *Ed.*

in the world and progressing from a particular to a particular, never arrives at a definitive closure of its chain of reasoning, and so insinuates a false idea of knowledge as wholly subordinate to life's other needs. Religion is the instrument of transcendent oppression. Both block Man's path to philosophical self-understanding, the path out of the world. Philosophy and its mimesis often live in the same person and constitute a truly schizophrenic split. Where the philosopher thinks he has reason to rejoice, it is often his double that reaps the fruit. Descartes' *malin génie*, the malicious demon who inspired his greatest discovery, is at the same time responsible for the obsession with certainty that deprived him of the fruit of his philosophizing, laying down instead the outlines of modern scientific efforts. A philosophical de monology, a conception of inner forces that rule the conflict between the world and the philosopher, would have to be posited beneath any history of philosophy that would be more than an index of doctrines.

A strange spectacle, this conflict! How can there be a conflict where there is no contact? There can be contact only where there is a shared field of movement—but that, it seems, is precisely what is missing here. The world can cancel the existence of the philosopher and, behold, philosophy *enters into history* by means of it! Nothing shows more clearly how inadequate such means are against the inner strength of philosophy. The reason why philosophy actually *must be* persecuted as soon as it crystallizes in its pure form is one that Nietzsche grasped profoundly in his invectives against Socrates—that the mundane projection of philosophy appears as a decline of life. Philosophy is a form of vital relaxation in which life ceases to be naively and spontaneously creative. Nietzsche coined a profound saying, "das Begreifen ist ein Ende,"[6] — Hence for Nietzsche not only our modern science, but even more so Socrates represents a disease. After all, present-day science as it actually exists is sustained by the idea of vital utility. The self-understanding of the scientist today differs only in emphasis, only quantitatively from the self-understanding of the technician. By contrast, for ancient philosophy, the sole goal is understanding. Before philosophy, humans want to know and think they know, but they do not want to *understand*. Pindar tells us that, "He is wise who knows much in virtue

---

[6] "Understanding is an ending". See also F. Nietzsche, *Nachlaß 1888*, VIII, 14/226/; Kritische Studienausgabe, Vol. 13, p. 398 (= *Wille zur Macht*, § 68). *Ed.*

of his nobility, while the tongues of those who merely *learned* vainly clack like an insolent flock of ravens against the divine bird of Zeus."[7] Nietzsche, too, was profoundly aware that as long as life retains its naive momentum, it does not understand, but merely commands. The unreflected life gives rise to myth and poetry, mighty visions that are the depositories of an immediate self-understanding of life in the form of models seen, of exalting events, of intoxicating, appealing enthusiasm. It also gives rise to men who live and die in order to show their greatness and their might to themselves and to others. Stand where the poet and the hero stand, and perhaps, for a moment, philosophical intellectualism will appear to you as petty bourgeois and plebeian. "Sokrates war Pöbel".[8] Part of Nietzsche's significance is that he can also speak against philosophy from the standpoint of the poet and the hero. The poet inspires the hero, the hero realizes the poet; their world is one of courage and danger while philosophy – so it seems – is a quest for comforting certainties. The philosopher seems to be an obstacle cast by life into the path of the hero to prevent him from charging off after his sovereign freedom.

Yet it was neither the poet nor the hero, but their parodies, their shadows, who executed Socrates. It was not spontaneous life in its full vitality, but its descendants, weakened and deprived of creative power of their own and anxious for that endangered inheritance, fearful for the sustenance of the spirit of their ancestors. The resistance of the unreflecting great intensifies in the resistance of the epigones of life into the spasm of revenge. Both are borne by the longing for unending life, understood as an inexhaustibility, and, in the case of authentic heroes, as an ongoing intensification. As if this inexhaustibility were to be taken for granted! As if it were enough to remove obstacles for life to flare up with greater strength! Does not the resistance to philosophy feed ultimately on the realization that philosophy has touched upon the essential moment of the finitude of life? Does not life retreat before the penetrating vision of philosophy which discovers in it "cet ennui absolu qui n'est en soi que la vie toute nue quand elle se regarde

---

[7] Pindaros, II. *Olymp.*, in: *Pindari carmina*, Leipzig – Berlin 1923, p. 98 n. *Ed.*

[8] "Socrates was riffraff". See also F. Nietzsche, *Götzendämmerung*. Das Problem des Sokrates 3. Kritische Studienaugabe, Vol. 6, p. 68. *Ed.*

clairement," "qui n'a d'autre substance que la vie meme, et d'autre cause seconde que la clairvoiyance du vivant?"[9] As Christianity would have the "next world" save life, as Buddha would by a dissolution in the universe, and socialism by the vision of a future society, Nietzsche would have the Superman save it. Might philosophy ultimately mean that life cannot be saved? Does not the comprehension of the threat of philosophy contain a certain, albeit repressed, understanding of philosophy? The whole struggle against the "intellectualism" of philosophy is a purposeful, even if not an intentional, misunderstanding. It is dangerous for life to understand its own inner sovereignty; the spontaneous thrust of life is outward, dwelling on things, goals, models. That life itself is the ultimate standard and creator, which is not a truth which life seeks, but rather one before which it hides.

Life unfolds naively as long as it projects the image of its own inner sovereignty before itself, as a reality in the world. In other words, naive life always has gods to whom it entrusts itself to save it from its factual finitude. Those gods can be models of perfect virtue suggested in a poetic vision, they can be hypostatized ideas of the philosophers, they can be hypostatized ideals, various conceptions of the force of nature as in Marx's "real humanism", which dreams of the man to come, who will not be subjected to things but rather will master them, or, on wholly different lines, in Nietzsche's conception of nature as brutal but grand, redeeming itself in the Superman as joy and creativity itself. The condition, though, is always that the gods should set down rules of behavior, set down an order and a goal and therewith a reliable salvation. In turn the condition of their authority is their reality, their power to determine what will come to pass. "Naivität, als ob Moral übrig bleibe, wenn der sanktionierende Gott fehlt!"[10] — It is not only paradoxical, but outright cynical not to believe in God, but still believe in his commandments. If the gods are salvation, they must be what ultimately determine all that happens and must make some way for

---

[9] "that absolute *ennui* which is itself nothing but life stripped bare when it sees itself clearly, whose substance is nothing but life itself together with the penetrating vision of the living?", Paul Valéry, *L' âme et la danse*, in: *Oeuvres*, II, Paris 1960, p. 167. *Ed.*

[10] "How naive, as if morality remained once the sanctioning God is gone!" F. Nietzsche, *Nachlaß 1885–1886*, VIII, 2/165/. Kritische Studienausgabe, vol. 12, p. 148 (= *Wille zur Macht*, § 253). *Ed.*

dealing with them possible, be it sustained by the pathos of love or of utility or of a will to power. Religion is based on mutuality: act as the gods command and the gods will reward you with your life. By contrast, what philosophy means was never stated as harshly as by Spinoza: "Qui Deum amat, conari non potest, ut Deus ipsum contra amet".[11] The pathos of philosophy is not a pathos of mutuality, but a one-sided pathos, moving from man to the suprahuman, but never back. I believe that it follows from the *idea* of philosophy that even philosophizing is not to be understood as the reward of the gods. A philosopher cannot tell people: philosophize and ye shall be saved. Philosophy is not salvation, either by merit or by grace. It is simply the individual calling of certain people and hence their inner necessity. Philosophizing brings joy to those who philosophize (in varied ways, to be sure, and entailing a hard, painful struggle with oneself for oneself), because there lives in it the passion to understand, as compelling as other grand human passions. I would interpret Aristotle's profound view of the identity of *hēdonē, theōria,* and *energeia theu* in this sense: life is the product of God's eternal perception and hence, as long as we live, there is always at least some joy in us. That, though, holds true for all life, not just for philosophy alone.

Philosophy is the court of ultimate clarity. It is born as the courage for the ultimate nature of what is, which naive life seeks to avoid. Part of the finitude of our actual life is to experience a need for some external support, for salvation. Salvation is the sustenance of our life by an external, absolute power. Philosophy, however, suggests a reversal of that situation: finitude cannot naively find "support" in absolute power simply because the absolute itself is wholly contained within the finite; the world itself is nothing other than the absolute in its naiveté. It is not possible to rely on the gods, because the absolute is not outside but within us. Man stands in a closer and more intimate relation to God than is either safe or pleasant. God within us sanctions our finitude. The absolutely creative God is not at the same time a commanding and a saving God. It is a God whom we cannot ask what to do. It is the philosopher's duty not to flinch at this thought, to "suffer the privilege

---

[11] "He who loves God cannot endeavor that God should love him in return." (*Ethics*, V, Proposition XIX). B. Spinoza, *Ethika ordine geometrico demonstrata*, V, prop. XIX., in: B. Spinoza, *Opera*, Heidelberg 1923–1925. *Ed.*

of his hidden glory."[12] The inmost secret of the purposeless philosophical God is perennial creation, devoid of will, of pathos, of drive, in secrecy with oneself.

If in addition to God there be gods, the philosopher says, they are neither in the last instance creative nor strictly infinite; they are mere products. But why descend from the peak once reached and long for what has been surpassed? Man does not need to create gods, if God incarnates himself in Man. Since Man is not charged with carrying out the external command of some god, he has no recourse but to seize his own freedom. Who, though, is free? What does a philosopher answer to this question, that much more pressing now since man has been deprived of all transcendent support? Will he not now be shamed by the inner emptiness of his principle; will not pale intellectualism manifest itself now in all its lifelessness?

Philosophy does not prescribe, it does not command. Philosophy is content to point to what is taking place in life before it and to clarify its significance. It is enough to point to the one thing that, without violence, without posturing and without spasms, makes life full without necessarily involving anything outside Man. It is the fact that every person can, with his decision, either grasp or miss the specific calling of his own. Such an authentic decision for one's calling does not calculate circumstances, possibilities and impossibilities, and Man grows as he encounters obstacles. It does not matter what Man outwardly is. His place in society, the accident of society, does not matter. The easier and more irresponsible a life is externally, the fewer opportunities for true substantiality within it. People removed from the frequently vulgar harshness of life conceal their guilt from themselves and it is not possible to say that they truly are, but that they only appear to be. The phenomenon to which philosophy can point, though, is that Man is able not only to seem to be, but also *to be*.

Thus what, in the last instance, philosophy appeals for is a heroic man. That is the word of philosophy spoken to Man. Heroism is not blind passion, love or revenge, ambition or will to power. Rather, it contains a calm clarity about the whole of life, an awareness that what I do is *for me* what I must do; the sole possible manner of my being in the world. Heroic being here, in the world, in this moment, does not

---

[12]   O. Březina, *Bolest člověka*, in: *Ruce*, Fr. Bílek, 1901. *Ed.*

wait for its confirmation and continuation in another world. Heroism accepts its own finitude. It is nothing other than the irrefutable proof of one's own substance, irreducible to mere circumstances, to the experiencing of the crossroads of this world. Philosophy then has the ability to purge the heroic man's self-understanding, letting him understand his faith not as a manifestation of the transcendent, but as a free human act. What is made manifest in this faith is not a god's transcendent command, but the principle of a man standing in a historical situation. Thus the comprehension of being, which philosophy arrives at when intellectually surpassing the world, is possible only with the genuine human being as represented by a free act. So we might, perhaps, express the ideal of a sovereign philosophy as that of a philosophy of heroism and a heroism of philosophy.

Reflection on Defeat

(1938)

We were defeated, and we can see all around the most painful moral consequences of catastrophe: a moral hangover, the seeking of culprits, the laying of blame upon others, a raging against principles and other abstractions, in short—disorientation, breakdown. Surrendering on this internal front is the most dangerous thing and can prevent us from making the most out of what can still be accomplished in the present moment: in the current mood, people are able to deny completely what was fought for and make that struggle not just useless but even ridiculous. We do not intend here to undertake a defense of those ideals – this is not the place for that – nor to accuse people or orientations; we only want to search our conscience, to look for a remedy.

The rule of the world is that the small must adapt. This does not mean that they must be minions of the big and not see truth, law, and justice. But they are not allowed to depend on truth, law, and justice – which, as we know, only the naive person sees quite simply and clearly – like on real powers of the world that in each and every case act for the benefit of those who force is attacking. The adaptation of the small means creative mental effort, in which old ideals are rejuvenated and new forces are sought in or for them. So we can suppose that, for example, the old ideals of freedom and human solidarity can or even must be brought into agreement with the collective pathos, which demands from individuals, ranks, classes, and parties the highest sacrifice. Above all, however, it is important that diligent and open-minded attention be dedicated to all of the forces of historical life, to those that are already active and those being born, so that they are contemplated and analyzed, and not judged under general slogans that conceive of them simplistically as axioms, but rather so that one's own opinion is corrected, deepened, and complemented with unceasing vigilance. This mental effort, which must be continuously carried out by whoever is in the position to decide about the most fundamental things, is a substantial part of what I understand as adaptation. The small must constantly be on guard employing their intellectual ability, their ability to comprehend things, when they are not granted the privilege of will.

Principally, it is far more difficult for the small to be unprejudiced and have an intellect that perceives accurately than for the big. The big are less threatened and thus have fewer reasons to indulge in the illusions, in which the small are easily entangled, especially if the big is not very familiar with the surrounding world and its complex relations. For both the big and the small wishing can be the mother of invention, but more depends on the wishes of the big. And yet the only way for the small to be saved is on this ground: whoever does not have enough flexibility here will have to engage in hand-to-hand combat, in which physical superiority wins unconditionally.

Such was our situation, where our so-called intelligentsia was a complete disappointment and was also utterly defeated. Unfortunately, along with them many superb, believing, disciplined people were defeated as well. We see that it is necessary to start recreating our "cultural" class from scratch. The current intelligentsia has been inflexible, snobbishly arrogant, rudely self-important, and often uneducated. In the best case, they are able only to drudge but never to do creative work. What a squandering of loyalty, of the diligent modesty of our small and smallest, whose trust the conceited "intelligentsia" so obviously abuses! It is an unleashed intelligentsia, which because of their immaturity requires control; in spite of all of the phrases, they do not have a vivid feeling of responsibility towards people, and the freedom that they use is not freedom of thought, because creative thought is foreign to them.

At all those who in their intractable intellectual immobility – which in the best case hides behind the façade of idealism, which deprived the nation of its state and compromised the future of their own children – we should shout: Do not be ashamed of becoming humble; it was not ideas and ideals that disappointed, but rather you yourselves, who were unable to apply them properly to reality; you all, we all, are guilty of the impotence we got ourselves into. Let us admit this so that the difficult moments we are living through can force our conscience to become aware of the crisis and help deepen our humility, help us to look ourselves in the eye and see how we really are; so that we can stand up as a nation courageous but humble, creative but quiet, hard-working but irreproachable, modest but with a lively spirit. The pain that now burns us might change into a profound gift, into a different fire, the one of which the famous song sings, when it mentions the heavenly host and the bright fire of the Holy Spirit.

Life in Balance, Life in Amplitude
(1939)

In the process of modern philosophical thought, insofar as Man is concerned, two typical and different attitudes have clearly crystallized. In these two attitudes there exists not only a different opinion about the essence of human being, but also about the role of philosophy in life. Although both of the types we are discussing are comprehensive titles for a great diversity of motivations and directions, prominent traits are shared that justify their aggregation. The first of these, which gravitates around the moral thinking that got the name of humanist ideology, comprehends Man as being essentially founded harmoniously; Man is called to happiness and a balance of all his forces. The process of history is at times slow and at other times faster and more energetic, but always tends as if by law towards that natural human aim of balance and harmony, for which everything is prepared and oriented in human nature. Man is a being that has not yet found the natural balance that is intrinsic to the life of all other living beings, namely a fixed form in which life runs its course. However, according to this orientation, this is just a provisional situation in life–there will come a time when human life will be so refined and organized that there will not be anything essentially unsteady and uncertain in this life, so that it will function ever more complex and artificial than the life of other creatures, but with certainty, straightforwardness, and accuracy. Opposite to this, the second type of philosophy of Man views him as a being that essentially cannot be encapsulated, can never be closed into a definitive form of life. On the contrary, Man appears to be most human and in his highest human function where the seemingly fixed form of life is scattered and where everything problematic, unsteady and extreme, which is hidden under the surface of normal living, is recovered.

Behind these two views stand two different attitudes towards life. The first type of philosophy is an expression of the common, of the leveling out of the everyday. The everyday with its normality, in which nothing substantial happens, in which there are no radical incisions, and when in the end the grayness of life triumphs over everything—this is the character of the understanding that we encounter here. Not that it would be a boring or bored philosophy; on the contrary it is very optimistic and sees life clearly, positively, and practically. But there exists in it – openly or secretly – a resistance to everything "not normal", extreme or sweeping, too constructive or inquisitive, fantastic or risky, that is contained in the nature of life and tempts it down dangerous paths. This philosophy holds on to the drab light of the usual day and places its "day view" against the "night view" of the experimentation of his opponent. Is it not quite clear that life has its own particular aims and rules, and that it is not necessary or even possible to penetrate deeper than what the everyday offers? Is it not clear that above all it is necessary to "cultiver son jardin"?[1] Is it not easy for people with common sense to agree about what is significant and practical, and leave to the madmen and the fantasists of this world their insignificant domain that is far from life? Life is a serious matter, but essentially simple. Let's live rationally, i.e., on the basis of deliberation, on the basis of all of our forces and powers, and we will reach the best that Man can ever possibly attain: harmony, balance, and bliss to that degree to which natural pains and losses allow Man. Those cases where life has not yet achieved harmony are due to the influence of mental, and mainly intellectual defects that are possible to get rid of through education, and to the influence of improper social institutions that are possible to get rid of through a rationally guided social process.

It is clear that this view corresponds to something very essential, some kind of fundamental need of our spirit. The task of rationally designed human coexistence seems to be easy in principle. It is difficult to understand why exactly people understand each other so little. The means and ends of human life seem to be so obvious. From the primitive hedonism of some of the parties in the epic poem of Gilgamesh, from the Indian and Chinese moral materialism or utilitarianism to the delicately refined modern systems of social evolution or social correction, this obviousness remains unchanged in the eyes of the re-

---

[1] Cf. Voltaire, *Candide,* ch. XXX. *Ed.*

presentatives of the view that is so often given the title of Enlightenment. In every person there is the inclination to think this way. This
inclination becomes permanent especially in those with strongly
rational characters and in enthusiasts of action when action is understood as a technical problem. But this also empowers the poetically
and morally enthusiastic characters precisely with its promise of universal harmony, justice, and happiness.

Yet there is something very unfavorable that argues against the
theses of this philosophy. How is it that our human reality corresponds
so terribly little to this philosophy and that always when Man attempts
to implement it in reality, he usually must return for a long time to the
thoughts and goals that he opposed in the beginning, against which he
went to fight? How is it that thoughts seemingly so obvious lead in
concrete situations to their opposites, that that which in these thoughts
inspires future happiness, leads to tragedy, and that which wants to
create a new life with serious meaning so easily covers up laxity and
moral decay?

Of course, to such a burning question the thinkers of this orientation
have an answer ready at hand. Or rather, they have a whole range of
answers that, *in concreto*, differ from each other, but what they have in
common is that the author's intention and the author's system does not
bear any blame for failure; reality had not yet reached the level that
would allow the theory to be applied, or reality will soon catch up with
the unfulfilled promises. They argue long and convincingly, they know
how *post festum* to diagnose in such detail all the causes and motifs and
incorporate them again and again into their schemes that were not able
to predict events, but curiously enough they easily know how to *absorb*
them so that the shaken trust rises again and resorts to new plans, new
hopes in which the old hopes are revived. Condorcet, in the middle of
the revolutionary terror, in which he himself would soon drown,
devises his *Sketch for a Historical Picture of the Progress of the Human Mind*[2] with his perspectives on infinite perfection, on the infinite
development of all positive abilities of the spirit by which Man heig-
htens his understanding of nature and the possibilities of ruling over it.
In the midst of the storm, in which the subsequent generation saw the

---

[2]   Jean Antoine Nicolas de Caritat, Marquis de Condorcet (1743–1794), *Es-
quisse d'un tableau historique des progres de l'esprit humain*, Paris 1795. *Ed.*

catastrophe of Enlightenment thought, he tried to fool himself, to forget himself in a dry phantasmagoric future that would correspond more to the demands of thought. Many social reformers, Saint-Simon for example, go from catastrophe to catastrophe retaining the structure of their optimism and continue to fill in new persons and conditions into it. How many times have so many Saint-Simonistes shed their skin (not mentioning the newer and more relevant people), especially Enfantin, so as to correct the continuous catastrophes and salvage the most essential aspects in which they experience the core of their own being. And in their humiliation, in this test to reach the roots of being, these figures take on a dimension for us that they had been missing so far, which was foreign to them and is only now imposed. They take on painful depths, they are something more than they admit to themselves, their enthusiasm obtains depth only now. That, which those who suffered with dignity did not see with the eye of the spirit that they trusted with the whole truthfulness of the soul, became obvious to them only through the hard oppressing blows of reality that willingly or not they had to respect.

For truly here the paths separate. Either Man is a finite, closed entity with a fixed form of life, and thus in principle history is a finished process, the searching for balance is justified as an aspiration for the aim of human society, all failures of our social, communal endeavors are only imperfections of a bad calculation that will finally somewhere come out right; or Man is essentially not something like that, he essentially cannot achieve balance and closure apart from by degradation, by not acknowledging himself. Fichte said, that our philosophy depends on how we are.[3] Pico de la Mirandola in his famous speech on human dignity[4] stated that God gave Man the freedom to choose and design the form of life he likes. However, the freedom of Man consists above all in the possibility to be or not be something more than Man *seems* to be. There exists a profound philosophical experience that Socrates and Plato imparted to all subsequent philosophical meditations. This is the *chorismos*, the divide between that which is and that which *only seems*

---

[3] J. G. Fichte, "Erste Einleitung in die Wissenschaftslehre" (1797), in: *Gesamtausgabe der Bayerischen Akademie der Wissenschaften*, Vol. I, 4: *Werke 1794–1796,* E. Lauth, Stuttgart – Bad Cannstadtt 1970, p. 195. *Ed.*

[4] G. Pico della Mirandola, *De hominis dignitate* (1486), Hamburg 1990. *Ed.*

to be, although this seeming originally concealed being and more strongly imposed itself than being did. Plato interpreted this difference as the divide between that which is understandable through reason and that which is accessible through the senses; for far-ranging speculative reasons, it is not possible to agree with Plato here. But the divide, the *chorismos*, is here and is manfested in a series of phenomena that are not of themselves proof, but that move us closer to understanding what it is about.

The first such phenomenon is drawn from history. History is not renewed so much by changing its material, but rather that the form of life of Man changes within it. Other aims, other sentiments, other interests, other realities continually appear in history. By rebound, some of these immensely sensitive and changeable dimensions even have an impact on that which is the most fixed and constant in life: on the natural givenness of the human vital needs and on the natural surroundings that now speak to us in symbolic speech and suggest another world.

It is possible to draw the second from the *comprehension* of history. Even the remote mental achievements and forms are accessible to our study, and although we may often be mistaken which is human, we might not always be able to disengage ourselves from ourselves and hence we may distort our object of study, we still very often succeed in *truly penetrating* into a foreign world, into dimensions so far hidden from us, and then it is like our eyes are opened: "in the secret [...] a new heaven is opened up, the sun of your day projects a shadow in a new direction".[5]

Another hint grows out of observation of oneself. Our life is not played out on level ground, but rather in various depths; each depth has its own conception of the others and knows about its own relation to the level ground of the average calm of life. Our mental development is not, figuratively speaking, a mere change of the objects in our living space, but rather movement from room to room, during which horizons into the indefinite open up from all sides.

A further hint is in the analysis of culture. Its *creation* was not and is not a mere attitude of indulgence and utility towards the richness of human life, but rather the fascination by the whole of the world always

---

[5]   O. Březina, *Čas,* in: *Ruce,* Praha 1901. *Ed.*

lives in human life (a more detailed analysis would be needed to show this), and this by a different way for each of the different cultural powers like science, philosophy, art, vita activa, and religion. This relation to the whole, this fascination with the whole—how else to construe this than as an essential relation of Man to that which is most universal, most comprehensive, elevated above everything limited and finite? What is finite itself can certainly never experience the infinite, the suprafinite and have a rapport with it.

So now perhaps it is possible to state at least certain indices that prepare the ground for a philosophy of amplitude. What does this philosophy mean? First of all, it is necessary to clarify what I understand to be a life in amplitude. I do not mean by this the *mere intensity* of life; a life in balance can be full of enthusiasm and pretend to be mysticism, of which we have so many examples from utopian socialism. For instance, the Saint-Simon sect provides tons of examples; its adherents talk about God, future life, metempsychosis; they mixed a foggy metaphysics with theories about free love and the first projects about economic planning; and they took it as especially important that they were considered to be a religious formation; and yet they could not dupe the provident eye of Carlyle who exposed their "religion" to be political propaganda. Amplitude is where Man leaves behind him the everyday level of the usual life of enchantment, the level of sober untruth that veils vision before the true heights and true dangers of our existence—there towards which Man heads with a calm expression and before which our timid finitude flees.

What does this necessary, diligent, reasonable everyday finitude want, what does it wish for? Nothing less than a guarantee of itself, a guarantee of a happy ending, a guarantee of the reasonable and practical purposefulness of living. Even though I will not be myself, my life will remain in the work I have done, passed down to those who follow. *Multaque pars mei vitabit Libitinam.*[6] The life of the individual and the society must have a kind of fixed center that it can be leaned upon. It is possible to close one's eyes to the nothingness that will someday embrace us completely, and give oneself over to the frenzy of work and activity. It is possible to have friends and opponents, to play an immense game with the lives of thousands and flip the switches of

---

6   Q. Horatius Flaccus, *Exegi monumentum,* in: *Carmina,* III, 30, 6–7. *Ed.*

history. It is possible to believe and hope that behind it all stands a benevolent force that sets all of the deficiencies of life right; one Russian philosopher formulated it recently that life made sense only then when it lasts long enough to be able to become worthy to be lived so that its subject can take it upon himself with dignity.

The timid finitude closes its eyes before the fact that life is bordered by two chasms, between which there exists a minute enclave of calm like a brief pause, which only makes sense in relation to that which is not a pause. The contingent person with his contingent aims has to become eternal, has to be victorious in the competition of history—this also is a "philosophy of history" that corresponds to this standpoint. Already in advance he experiences the satisfaction of the victory that will never be real for him, and in this way he projects himself so far beyond himself, far outside of himself. This self-elongation, self-projection seems to be something reasonable and obvious: it makes possible organized and noble work that then gives one the impression that he is the lord over his own history, that he fights for ideas, that he lives in his empirical life a kind of divine drama, in which empirical Man is only the surface layer of a more profound divine life.

Furthermore, the average life yearns to be spared the shaking that we seemingly encounter contingently, which signifies a test, loss, pain, which in the program of practical life that is arranged according to plans and aims for successes signifies sheer deficit. It yearns for life to be arranged as practicaly as possible, with excluding most of these deficits. This average life does not doubt that its apparent satisfaction is the real fullness of life. It seeks to elude that which, in spite of all official optimism, it grasps as its inner deficit which awaits the time that the stream of life would reach the next vortex when the deficit becomes a real catastrophe. Life knows about its inner weakness and its first reaction is to elude its consequences.

The philosophy of amplitude is one that is conscious that life must in each moment bear the entire weight of the world and accepts this duty. The philosopher does not want to look for and construct artificial paradises that transform the human future, and does not want to awake banal hopes. He attempts to make the world easy by a different method.

He starts from the view that the *life in amplitude* is a fact. We experience the life in amplitude when we extricate ourselves from the *life in enclave* and go, as Jaspers says, to the boundaries of our existence.

(This *advancing to the boundaries* as a thought inspiring the modern philosophy of existence is correct and positive. However, the carrying out of this thought in existential philosophy, e.g., in Jaspers, is not positive enough—it is too hesitant.)

The boundaries, to which Man is constricted, are of two types. On the one hand, there is physical weakness and Man's limitation of will, manifesting in physical pain, misery, disease, oppression, guilt, and death. This always possible and, in this possibility, constantly present deficit is not contingent for Man. If these possibilities did not exist, Man would not be what he is in his essence. The ability to suffer is positive. This exists also in animals, but Man suffers more and deeper. This greater suffering comes from a higher consciousness. The higher consciousness is a second, inner boundary that is inside us deeper than we ourselves are: that overcoming of the moment, that advancing to the universal horizon, which lives in us and allows us to encounter reality, which we deal with and that never completely fulfills us. The unified structure of the experienced world is something different than a collection of physical and mental realities. And this structure is the reason why the more we hope and the clearer we see life, consequently also the more we suffer.

Living in amplitude means a *test* of oneself and a *protest*. In amplitude, Man is tested by exposing himself to the extreme possibilities that are mere abstract, distant possibilities for the common life, and protests against those that are usual and obvious. Strangeness and peculiarity, however, are not the motives here since the pursuit of them is something so common. Man reaches amplitude under the fascinating impression of the boundaries that encircle his life. He must face these boundaries, if he searches for *truth*. If we want truth, we are not allowed to look for it only in the shallows, we are not allowed to be fascinated by the calm of ordinary harmony; we must let grow in ourselves the uncomfortable, the irreconcilable, the mysterious, before which the common life closes its eyes and crosses over to the order of the day.

The existence in amplitude often gives to the usual consciousness the impression of unnaturalness, disease, spasms, which the healthy, normal person cannot handle. Of course, there are various types of such a life: Socrates does not give the impression of being spasmodic, and yet his life rose to heights practically unattainable; in Pascal there is not only the vehemence of the attacker and heroic defender, but also a mystical calmness. But Kierkegaard, with his eternal reflection, with his tense dialectic gives the impression of inhuman ice; Nietzsche the impression of convulsion; Dostojevsky the impression of ongoing crisis. All of them are in some way inaccessible; we feel them protrude from our warm surroundings into the icy vacuum. To endure this position, to truly undergo it, is a strange phenomenon that is difficult to understand; we truly see that they often completely burn up rather than abandoning this position and descending—and in this position they protest vigorously against the all too human illusions, against the naive paradises of the huddled, "harmonic" souls, against those life dreams in the calm, untroubled tracks of employment, work, usual obligations, utility, harmony, and happiness. They also look for their paradise, but it is not a paradise of closed, but rather open eyes.

By taking off into amplitude, they employ the freedom inherent to Man. Only by doing this, they make the potential freedom real, since only by acting can they attain that which Man *truly is*, and thus that which *he truly can be*. That is how they realize the *chorismos*, the chasm between the two orientations of humanity, between the path of all matter and the narrow path of the spirit.

For the spirit is not, as so often it is supposed by those who depict it in a too convenient way, living from the ready-made. It is not the mere occupation with the sublime or immaterial, but rather it is a relation to the world, living from comprehending the world as a whole, as attained in amplitude. This is an universal interpretation, coming from a light ignited not intellectually, but from the life of the spirit striking against the hard stones of our borders.

He who takes such a possibility upon himself is free in a profound sense. He frees himself of the mere seeming that nails us to deep weaknesses, to futile hopes. The awoken freedom revealed what seemed to be as seeming and in accepting the danger acquired only now its full safety, acquired for Man a life out of his own roots, out of his own foundation. Because in this, in the struggle for freedom, in the struggle with himself, Man took possession of himself, of the deepest that he has in himself or that he is able to reach. In this spark, this new life appears to him.

Already from the time of Rohde,[7] it has been well known that the Greek epos – which formulated a bright world of Olympic gods and

---

[7] Erwin Rohde (1845–1898), *German classical philologist*. See also E. Roh-

independent, courageous, free people – was an act of liberation from the dark power of the chthonic myth; more recently Bäumler made an attempt to show Greek tragedy in a similar light.[8] But also Greek philosophy, with its principle of participation in ideas, of the getting under control of being by means of idea, is essentially a way to endure when coming face to face with the panic of myth and the shallowness of popular religion. Christianity meant and means a descent into the sphere of pain and guilt, at the retrieval of their meaning—and again here a new world spreads out in front of our eyes. This all is only a crude illustration of what we want to say here: in real amplitude Man does not only get under control his external, but also his internal boundaries. There does not exist any true spiritual activity arising only from the sphere of ideas. Our internal border, the world that lives within us, does not cause us pain. However, pain, brought under control and endured in amplitude, teaches us to discover the world and shows us that we are free in interpreting its meaning.

Pain casts or can cast us into that dimension that is not closed to us, to the dimension of our own depth, which cannot be plundered. For this discovering of the inner, altered light, it is possible even to love pain, which is so much deeper and greater than the inebriation from power and success. The essence of humanity is not to feel fulfilled by finiteness. But power, success, and "mundane" greatness are finite things. Crude souls can speak about spiritual imitations of mundane successes, about the sour grapes of the world. But he who has been transformed by pain, no longer has a yearning for the vulgar bliss and tough power of the day, as long as he does not fall down to an entirely different level. He praises that which hindered him from succumbing to the common emptiness and aimlessness that is called the desire for power and happiness. Therefore, all of the true lovers of the eternal and infinite are above all those who have gone through adversity and pain. We take adversity here in its literal meaning of opposing the spontaneous huddling of human nature, going against our illusions, against our beloved fears, fed by secret wishes, against our superstitions.

de, *Psyche. Seelenkult und Unsterblickkeitsglaube der Griechen*, Vol. I–II, Freiburg im B. 1890–1894. *Ed.*

[8] Alfred Bäumler, "Preface" in: F. Nietzsche, *Die Geburt der Tragödie*, Stuttgart 1955. *Ed.*

The *philosophy* of amplitude follows the whole play of human experiences, standpoints, and life attitudes, it warns against the usual illusions and inspires the love for the eternal—this love alive in this philosophy.

Ideology and Life in the Idea

(1946)

In the period between the two wars, there was much debate about how Man has become more problematic for himself than ever before. During this period, the contemporary understanding of Man had broken apart, and out of this different "ideas of Man" had allegedly emerged. Thus, theory has been marked by disunity, while at the same time a deeper crisis has been played out in *praxis*. It is evident that from the First World War up to today one of these ideas of Man is still in crisis; i.e., the idea of Man which can be called specifically modern, which has its roots in Enlightenment thought on nature and human nature, and out of which humankind's programs and ideals have successively emerged since 1715 until today.

When discussing concept and idea, we need to distinguish specifically between the two. The concept of Man is a theory about him, a theory that stands alongside other theories; it is a theory, as it does not engage us. As such a concept can become myth or ideology, which do engage, which accommodates these tendencies, needs, and forces that lay dormant within us to lead, direct, and draw them together for the needs of social action.

However, ideology – although it engages, conceptually grasps, and binds us – seizes Man externally, like certain forces in the overall complex of forces. Forces such as what is required to achieve a certain social aim that is solely valuable and valid; so that everything else, not the least of which is the will and activity of the individual, acquires its significance from this aim alone. An idea is something distinct from this: an idea must be embodied, and this embodiment in life concerns our innermost personal core and can never be indifferent towards this inner core. An idea appeals to us, not so that we put ourselves "at the service of the Idea", but rather to be in the Idea, to exist in the Idea.

From one war to the other, we have observed an intensifying crisis in Man's contemplation of Man—or, putting it more profoundly, in the way Man relates to himself. Although the great social movements, whose roots lie in the Enlightenment concept of human nature, still have the lead, uncertainties are emerging: both theoretical uncertainties and political and moral uncertainties. The great crisis of social humanism is linked to the disappointment that was produced by the world war and even the peace. Fascism, which drives the crisis to extremes, was no doubt destroyed by the war. But every major war leads to crises of confidence, as we saw in the First World War, and as is still felt to a large extent even today. We must ask: What exactly is in crisis? Towards what is this distrust directed? What has withstood the crisis and remains after it? Is it the concept of Man, is it the Idea, or is it ideology? Is there in all honesty something more remaining today than absolute realism in the relation to Man, a lack of total confidence in everything that would want to exceed our purely material relation to Man?

In the European West, the moral consequences of the First World War led to a crisis of confidence in liberal ideals: the ideals of political freedom, democracy, and national self-determination. Although the side that espoused these ideals won, the war itself, the fact that the war happened, was a serious indictment against these ideals in the eyes of the wider public. Why were they not able to prevent the war? Why were they not able to prevent the preying off the hardship and destitution of millions? During this, both the common people and the elite vividly felt that something had remained intact beyond this conflict marked by its obscurities and impurity. Thus many heads also turned toward the social ideal dawning in the East. The youth in the West as well as here certainly felt this, as can be seen in our post-war literature, with its prevalence of social motifs and radical social orientations. In addition to these, the concept of Man, as presented in scientific socialism, penetrated society into society: a concept that was not meant to be just an inert theory, but an effective means of class struggle. So the moral crisis of the First World War was not universal in character; it did not affect all of humanism, given that, on the contrary, the crisis celebrated and gave prominence to humanism's social form.

But socialism is at once an idea, an ideology, and a concept of Man. The great socialist movements contain all these elements without differentiating between them. Socialism appeals to Man internally; but at the same time it views him externally like a thing among things, a force among forces, and it is an ideology that organizes these forces. The effects of ideology have their own special laws that are at times paradoxical in nature. One such law is that, under certain circumstances, the more fatalistic, the more objectivistic, a particular ideology's character is, the more vigorous and resolute it acts. Examples are well known: Muslim fatalism, as the drive in the struggle against the infidels; the fatalism of God's chosen flock, as with the Hussites in Tábor, Reformation fatalism, with its preordained "callings" and the need to "prove oneself" through life. It is also clear, however, that, if a crisis is to be avoided, each ideology must constantly be supervised by the Idea; we observe the crisis, after all, with the effects of each ideology. The original meaning of the whole doctrine is often forgotten: the Prophet's aggressive conquering thought, the Christian teachings on love, the salvation of one's soul (which gave meaning to the disregard for oneself, to the defense against spiritual violence, and to the morality of work and success in life), so that they remained only as means that can also be used for other purposes. It is generally known that this is where the roots of the heterogeneity of historical purposes that is so often discussed lie. In socialism, there is also a peculiar fatalistic aspect, collectivistic objectivism, which sees the individual as merely the instrument of a collective act, and whose laws absolutely direct and control the individual. In this Man is purely the object of action and organization. It is not our task here to explore the real reasons why such thinking, in which Man is regarded as merely the object of the historical process, could give rise to false collectivisms, i.e., collectivisms without the Idea, with just a factual-political meaning. It is true that these false collectivisms developed and were fundamentally successful in certain societies. It is true that they were capable of mobilizing even those forces of Man that, in the pure socialistic impulse, were not engaged: not just "revolution" and "the whole", but also the irrational impulses of xenophobia and racial and national origin. And although false collectivisms intended to destroy socialism, only by means of appropriating those elements of socialist ideology that make it possible to lead and organize the masses. A false socialism, a false revolutionary *pathos*, a false fraternity in opposition to other nations and races were able to emerge. And they were capable of control so powerful that people died for it and did not hesitate to mobilize the entire social reality to ensure that it was enforced. This is a shaking experience. This means, among other things, that there was something missing from the socialism in Italy and Germany, where the socialist movement were nevertheless extremely strong. But this also means that the struggle against the false mimicries of the socialist idea cannot be waged just on an ideological level. Ideology can be strong or weak; ideology can prevail or be suppressed; people can believe in it or not; they can transform it and misuse it for their own purposes. They cannot however live in it completely; they cannot realize it in themselves nor realize themselves through it. Something else is needed for this. Exterior successes and failures can never be fully convincing in so far as life decisions are concerned—about where is the real, where is the ultimate human truth. And as long as people judge things only ideologically, not in relation to the Idea, there is no way out of relativism and scepticism.

Amidst this situation the Second World War arrived. Unlike the First World War, which was not as radical, everything down to its naked, physical roots was engaged in this war. It was no longer a war bound within the limits of a clear political plan and budget. It also was not a war that would compromise only the old ideologies that had grown more or less out of date, thus leaving people a certain intellectual reserve untouched by the fight. Everything was cast into the struggle. The phrase promoted in Germany was victory "at any price", i.e., at the price of any kind of use or abuse of Man. On the other hand, even though these means were not used, the resolution to win was no less, and the demands on what the individual was required to sacrifice for society were almost unlimited. Nothing connected; nothing bridged the antithesis of the two contenders any longer, as the concept of socialism had at the end of the First World War. The falseness showed its strength to such a degree that it was necessary to go as far as physically breaking the roots of evil; and the mortal hatred of the enemy goes way beyond the grave. Thus there seems to be no grand conception connecting them as human beings, valid for everyone, a single hope, to which everyone would have the same right to look up. Given that each political conception in this conflict used very extreme tactical means, a sceptical impression was able to rise to the surface, questioning where the evolution was leading to and to what degree the original purity of the doctrines was still upheld.

It would be very dangerous if, under these circumstances, any such extremely widespread conviction, in which Man is merely a minute item in the general accounting of nature, were to assert itself more today. If this conviction would be true, then the problem of human society is a mere technical and tactical problem; and this is how fascism, in its different varieties, assessed the question of political forces. Any means is technically good if it is effective; and the effect depends on whether we secure for ourselves the safe mastery of available forces. Man is such a force, controllable from without as well as from within: take care of his economic security, give him a place within the mass self-consciousness, organize his mind with propaganda and his recreation and entertainment with the appropriate measures, and he will belong to you completely, and he will even think that he is free and that all of this is the authentic realization of Man. Whoever does not fit in is dealt with as a detrimental, useless force—and is necessarily ruthlessly neutralized. I think that the expansion of such an ideology must always again lead to similar attempts at fascism, maybe more clever and more successful, but essentially always to similarly humanly desperate attempts, since there is no place in them for the Idea.

Ideology, as a practised theory, cannot alone wrench itself out of the limits of the logic of theory, a logic that looks upon its object from the exterior. Conversely, the logic of the Idea has the peculiarity that it is not merely the "contemplation of things", but rather an identification with the Idea. We find such logic in its classical specimen in Socrates, who contemplates what is good, with the result that he does not state the Good (on the contrary, a definition simply stating what the Good is somehow continuously eludes his contemplation), but that he becomes good—the Good is established in life and thought themselves. However, the Idea of Man is essentially continuously the same, only the historical situation in which it is realized changes, only the main front against which the Idea resists is always different. The Idea is human freedom; the Idea of Man is the idea of human freedom. To look upon Man purely materially will always be the absolute opposite of the Idea. That is why socialism is an idea: it asserts and embodies human freedom in contrast to economic oppression and the exploitation of man by man. But it is consequently also in irrepressible tension with naturalistic ideology. According to the logic of the Idea, Man is able to live by his own resources; according to factual logic, only from the general context of things. According to one, the human world is an autonomous, self-purposive world of fraternal relations; according to the other, only a reflection of the material order. According to the first, the human world is the origin of all value, thus the heaviest; according to the second, the absolute annihilation of worth, thus the lightest. One knows the difference between what is allowed and what is not; the other only knows the difference between what is and what is not possible to carry out. The difference in this double logic is also the reason for what many have felt to be a peculiar discrepancy in modern socialism, namely, the consecration of the means by the end. The neutrality of means is valid solely in factual logic, since they are just the causes of material consequences and do not depend on anything else except the effect; in the logic of the Idea this is not valid since it is not the mere factual result that is important here, but rather the realization of Man; that Man vitally, internally merges with the Idea, which opens up to him; and it is clear in this that Man cannot realize the Idea in himself if he develops characteristics and forces that are in fundamental contradiction with the Idea; if humanity is realized by inhuman violence, truth and honesty by silencing and lying, fraternity by control from without as well as within. Not that it would not be possible to use force and violence at all: surely it is sometimes necessary to kill and execute, but that in itself is not yet inhuman. But not even in the struggle with the adversary is Man allowed to be a mere thing, a mere force, as the will to use *any* means claims. To the logic of the Idea belongs Socrates' famous sentence that it is better to suffer wrongdoing (although this does not mean that it is good in itself!) than to do wrongdoing; to the logic of the Idea belongs the consciousness of the responsible, in that they do not want privileges for themselves; to the logic of the Idea belongs the *inner* significance of the highest sacrifice; the fact that what is a sheer loss from an external viewpoint, can be inner fulfilment (regardless of all external purposes, such as the kind of response that death for the Idea and its propagandistic significance awakens).

There is no doubt that the primary theoreticians of socialism knew well what the logic of the Idea demands. Marx's celebrated statement that the point is not to construe the world, but change it, shows that what concerned them was not "pure theory" but rather a real transformation in the being of Man. And the famous objection to metaphysics that it delays the urgent, revolutionary task shows that they put the necessity of realizing the Idea over the mere concept, which distances itself from the object to which it is indifferent. But the logic of the Idea is a difficult, unresolved philosophical problem: its resolution by means of the "dialectical method", i.e., a logic other than formal but nonetheless objective and factual, is in conflict with the essential inwardness of the logic of the Idea. Although the dialectical method spans the difference between present and future, individual and social reality, it transfers the entire process of the Idea out of human inwardness to the things themselves. Thus the freedom of Man is something meta-human. It is realized somehow outside of Man by a process at the end of which stands the freedom of Man as a future goal and not as this realization process itself.

And this is where, despite the experiences, or even actually because of the experiences of the last war, the Idea remains valid – the Idea as a manifestation of the inner core, a manifestation of inner freedom. It is easy to reproach such a conception for its abstractness, unrealness, and illusiveness, but nothing is less justified. Never has the cold, statistical reality of the social activities that comprise been as cynically widespread as it is now: from reports about the tens of thousands of lives a single day of battle claims, the newspaper articles about mass graves, the "liquidation" of millions in camps, the news about shortages, hunger, and epidemics which affect or will affect entire vast societies. All of us are accustomed to thinking this way, even those who were not behind the big or small control panels. We all experienced and are experiencing how much in this world Man has become a mere object of forces that extend beyond him. Out of the promised, final happy-endings to world events, at the end of the war we were able just to sigh with relief over the fact that the worst of the threats we had been faced ultimately never occurred. But in the course of the fury of war there were not even these consolations, and did this mean possibly the abdication of Man? The experiencing was difficult and rough, but not meaningless. What was lived through in the midst of the tempest was the resoluteness in everything on the one hand, and the immeasurable insignificance of an individual human life, its extreme "lightness" on the other hand. The individual has moved between these positions that somehow essentially go together: on the one hand, an insignificant material component, on the other something that cannot be broken internally but only externally eliminated. Only this measuring of the external by the internal and of the internal by the external shows the whole harshness and unavoidability of the war struggle. So once again we return to the concept of the inner core: has the inner core only appeared here and only as "a force seen from within"? However, how is it possible – given what we have witnessed, in spite of its frailty – that right in the fall, in sacrifice, in the *middle* of the struggle, without the result having been attained, and thus without justification by this result, Man can be glorified and fulfilled? From this point of view, even this immense lightness and fragility of human factual existence acquires special meaning. This is not just an external coincidence; this is the limit beyond which it is no longer possible to catch man—and consequently to pursue, to persecute him; the limit on which he must remain standing. And he who survives on the limit unbroken, and not deprived of his ultimate meaning, has fulfilled himself as much as it is at all possible for Man: he has remained free. We experience with him *this* genuine inner integrity by being aware of our own weakness, chaoticness, and ashamedness. Hence also the strange weakness and futility of all celebrations and remembrances after the fact; in the safe shadow of the attained result, the greater part of the truthfulness of those lives that are fulfilled in the deeper sense is lost.

Ideology, programs, thoughts, notions, and concepts come and go; the Idea of Man remains. But this Idea is neither a scholarly creation of constructive reason nor a fairytale of some kind of other world. It is what eternally remains with Man whenever the situation into which he is put appears to him as a fundamental threat to his entire inner being. This could not even not illuminate this war. We also want the Idea to illuminate this peace and its struggle for a new Man, for the rebuilding of his social relationships. Thus let everything that happens in this direction be judged by this Idea!

The Spiritual Person and the Intellectual[1]

(1975)

What I would like to present to you today is not a continuation of the interpretations that I have already given here [2] It is rather a reflection on what a spiritual person is and what an intellectual is, and the difference between them; on what the spiritual life is and culture is, and the difference between them; and on what the situation of the spiritual person is in the world—especially in *today's* world.

I think that today the term "spiritual person" does not sound very pleasant. It sounds spiritualist in some way and nowadays we tend to dislike such phrases. But does there exist a better expression for what I have in mind? Take it as a makeshift phrase of necessity. Anyone who has a better terminological proposal should kindly let me know.

It is very important to realize clearly that concealed within what is commonly called a person of intellect, a person of intelligence, an intellectual, there are two completely different things, which are nevertheless connected to each other, perhaps like a thing and its shadow and also – if we use the words of the person who first attempted to clarify this difference – like reality and its distorted image. This is because, on the one hand, we have the intellectual, the cultural actor, and possibly the creator as a certain social reality, which we can objectively define and analyze—sociologically: this is a person who has a certain education, particular skills, some certificates eventually, and on the basis of this he develops a specific activity from which he understandably derives a livelihood. So he earns a living just like anybody else by performing some other kind of activity—the way a cobbler earns a living making shoes, a worker by going to a factory; so,

---

[1] Transcribed from a tape recording by Ivan Chvatík. *Ed.*

[2] Patočka gave this lecture just after he presented the third seminar of the Heretical Essays on 11 April 1975. *Ed.*

too, the writer makes his living by writing on paper, and what he creates is printed, sold, bought, and enters into the economic sphere, etc. Naturally this is described in only very rough terms; of course, this means of livelihood has its own history and incorporation in other human activities...

And what about the other? This is not as simple and self-evident. It is not a matter that we could define externally by such statements and observations that these people do this or that. The majority of these so-called spiritual people also write something on paper and develop a particular activity like the others—like those who make a living through culture: externally it looks completely the same, there is no difference. They are writers like other writers, they are teachers like other teachers, they lecture like other lecturers, etc. Thus, in regard to this aspect, I would say, *we cannot distinguish between them.* That is precisely the problem we are faced with here. And yet there exists an absolutely profound difference. It was Plato who first noticed something of this sort: the terrible difference between a person like Socrates and a person like Pròtagoràs or Hippiàs and all those other wonderful virtuosi, who knew how to do so many things and who dazzled so wonderfully as teachers and as skillful money-makers. Where does this difference lie?

Plato endeavored throughout his entire intellectual life to somehow define this difference. He dedicated his greatest efforts and the majority of his works to this endeavor, and the question remains as to whether he was successful in clearly and sharply defining this difference, despite the fact that the dialogue containing the most deeply elaborated problematic of this duplicity – the *Sophist* – is a mature work of Plato's wisdom. This dialogue (all of you have no doubt read it or heard about it) shows how this other, the sophist – the person of intelligence, the intellectual, the cultural person – how difficult it is to grasp him, how he is always hidden. Always when we suppose that we have grasped him in some way, he is already somewhere else.

This is strange, isn't it? Plato sets out from the view that the figure of the spiritual person is clear and real, and that the sophist is someone who hides in the shadow of this bright figure. This is a slightly different point of departure from mine today: I am saying that the cultural person is something self-evident; after all, he performs certain activities which can be externally stated, described, and defined – sociologically, economically, etc. – whereas the spiritual person, so it seems to me, is a horrible problem.

Precisely because he was such a deeply spiritual person and this spirituality was close and obvious to him, Plato reversed this.

But let us return to our initial position. How can we shed light on what a spiritual person is? I shall try to proceed from the words of a great modern philosopher who attempted to define a certain type of spiritual life, namely philosophy, by saying: philosophy is a world inverted.[3]

In what sense is it inverted? In what sense does the philosopher invert the reality of other people, of those who are not – as I tried to say – spiritual people?

The philosopher differs from others in that the world, for him, is not self-evident. We all live in a world that is given to us, that is open to us, and that we take as reality. This reality is something that is simply here and that we take as an absolute matter-of-course as a reliable base on which we move without difficulty. Moreover, our life in the world is also such a matter-of-course. All of our reactions we learned, all of the objects around us we learned to name on the basis of a language that we adopted, all of our opinions we have from tradition, all of our thoughts we have from school: so everything is, so to say, prescribed for us, and whenever we show a little of our own initiative, we also adhere to something clear and self-evident. And most of the time, if we don't encounter any great difficulty and unpleasantness, then that is enough; we do not need anything more. Life thus adopted does not encounter any obstacles.

The experiences, that show us that precisely this whole way of seeing the world as self-evident and adopted is something that *disappoints*, something exposed to negative outcomes, are rare; they are rare, but in the end everyone encounters them in one form or another. We see that the people with whom we live together, act together, work together, think together, learn together, that precisely these people – even we ourselves – are inconsistent, that they are disunited, and that they live in contradiction; we see that they betray each other, that their life projects disappoint them, that they abandon their former beliefs.

---

[3]   G. W. F Hegel, *Werke*, Vol. 2; *Jenaer Schriften*, Frankfurt a. M. 1969–1971, p. 182. *Ed.*

There are, however, even harsher experiences. There are experiences like the unexpected end of life, death, experiences of the collapse of entire societies. These are experiences that you all know from your childhood, or that those of us know who have been through these experiences several times during our lives. They all suddenly show that life, which looked so obvious, in reality is somehow problematic, that something is in disarray, that something is not in order. Our original attitude is that *it is in order*, that all of these minute unpleasantries, disagreements, and incongruities have no significance and that it is possible to get over them. For after all, the world at every moment says something to us: our actions are nothing other than an answer to the fact that the world says something to us; that things have meaning for us, that they challenge us to do something, and we answer them. And if we were to really, consistently follow this negative that suddenly makes itself heard, if we were to go after it consistently, that would no doubt mean that nothing will say anything to us, also nothing will challenge us to some kind of activity, to some kind of reaction and/or action, and as a result we will remain in a vacuum, we will be stuck in a kind of emptiness. It is not possible to live in that! And yet *here*, in this lies the beginning of spiritual life.

I have already mentioned Plato several times: Plato presents the origin of spiritual life in the figure of Socrates. And Socrates' spiritual life consists in his attempting to feel out, through conversing with other people, whether these people and *he himself* are capable – in the most diverse questions of life, in the simplest as well as more complicated – of maintaining unity within themselves; whether they are able to be consistent; whether that which they take as given is truly sufficient for the life that is identical with itself, in accord with itself; whether these people are truly what they suppose themselves to be; and whether their supposedly united figure does not collapse in mere conversation. And the experience that Socrates creates, the result at which he arrives by quite simple methods, by quite simple cleverness that still is successful in avoiding this problematicity, is that *nowhere* does he come across something like a real, firm character who can realize his own identity. And Socrates himself does not pretend to be the kind of person who would know how to carry this out. He only wants this, he only goes towards this, he only strives for this. *He is only on a quest.* And that is the most important thing: the spiritual person is he who is, in a way, *on a quest*. He knows about these negative experiences, he never loses sight of them. He is unlike the common person, who seeks to forget them, who seeks to get past them by means of instinct, for life works itself out; he can *already* bear this life somehow; he *already* has a cure for these problems. Whereas this is not true for the spiritual person: precisely the spiritual person exposes himself *to these experiences*, and his life consists in being thus exposed.

To be thus exposed to the negative, to create a special life scheme, means in a certain sense a completely *new* life. While the usual life exists in presumed self-evidence and security and is directed towards such security, dismissing incongruities and negatives, the new life is lived from these negatives. And this means that everything has a different keynote, a different value than in this unfragmented, straightforward, and naive life.

I named the kind of life experiences that no one can avoid and that everyone seeks at first to somehow evade; but under these surface experiences there are, I would say, experiences that are in a certain sense deep. These are experiences that show something like the peculiarity, the strange wonderment of our situation—that *we are* at all and that *the world is*, that this *is not* self-evident, that there is something like an amazing wonder, that things *appear* to us and that we ourselves are among them. This wonderment! This is *"divné"*[4]: this word contains *"wonder"*. We wonder: to wonder means not to accept anything as self-evident, to stand still, to stop oneself, not to go further in one's quest, to stop functioning. An obstacle. Such an immense obstacle over which we may stumble so that we will never return. And truly, to stumble over this thing means never to return.

When I wonder in this way—it is strange, isn't it? Materially the world is completely the same as before, there are the same things, the same surroundings, the same chairs and tables, people and stars, and nevertheless there is something here *completely* changed. No *new* thing was discovered, no new reality, but something was discovered that is not any *thing*, not a reality, namely, that this everything *is*. But that everything *is*, is not any kind of thing.

---

[4] This Czech word means peculiar or strange. The root of the word is "div", which means wonder. Patočka is showing the etymological relationship between wonder and what is regarded as strange. *Ed.*

This new manner of life consists, then, in our being able to live in such a way that we do not accept life simply, but rather we accept its *problematicity*. From this moment on, this is our base; it is that in which we live and breathe. This also means that, from this moment on, we cannot accept anything as a finished and given thing, we cannot rely on anything; everything we accepted as self-evident is not self-evident; everything we know is prejudice.

There are several features, which I attempted to put my finger on: not ignoring negative experiences, but on the contrary settling into them; problematizing the usual; creating a new life *possibility* from within this open sphere. To live not on firm ground, but rather on something that moves; to live in *unanchoredness*. You will say to me: what you are saying here might concern philosophy, but it does not touch upon everything we normally call a spiritual life—as the spiritual life we count art and religion and also the active life, a life, let's say, of sacrifice, devotion, and responsibility, and eventually something like the creation of certain social institutions, like law, etc. All of this is the spiritual life after all!

This objection is fully justified, but in all of these areas (this would be possible to prove, but I do not intend to elaborate on it too broadly here) there is the identical difference, the difference between, on the one hand, a certain activity that can be externally described, stated as a certain fact, and introduced into other factual contexts, and, on the other hand, the way people live and act who problematize in these areas.

To make this more concrete, I could cite the example of poetry: think about the poetry of Homer, commonly considered as naive, seemingly unfragmented, and presenting a picture of life that is seemingly so clear and naive. However, in reality we know that Homer's epic is the embodiment of the immense experience of the post-Mycenaean era, which lived through the decline of the age of heroes, and that all of this poetry is a reflection on the experience of a certain collapse of an epoch. And who can think about Homer without calling to mind the great theater at the end of *the Iliad*, the colossal scene towards the end where Achilles and Priam stand across from each other – these two who destroyed each other so perfectly – and speak together in such an instant of human unanchoredness, when it is as if life is a cease-fire between two battles, and in this moment, each comes to know the other as that which Man in reality is. And think about the figure of Achilles himself—a person who chooses precisely this short and glorious life! Something directed *against* the direction of usual life, something that belongs to the foundation of Greek political sentiment.

Or Dante, who sees life "here" through life "there"—our life, here, this life which we live in this unfragmentedness, *through* that life which he recognizes by a pilgrimage to the *other* world.

Or Rilke, who lives in a continual exchange between this life and the other world—this life, which continually disappears somewhere and to which that *from whence* it came and *whither* it again departs continually speaks.

Essentially, all of philosophy is nothing other than the development of this problematicity as great thinkers have expressed and grasped it. The struggle to extract out of this problematicity something that emerges from it; to find a firm shore, but then again problematize that which emerges as a shore. This is that primal Greek wisdom expressed in the words "Thunderbolt steers all things"[5]: the flash that reveals *the light of dawn* in the darkness but at the same time reveals *the darkness*—the emerging of entirety, but from out of the darkness that belongs to it and which this lightning only tears through, but does not overcome.

And then, in Antiquity, where Socrates was the role model, Plato made an immense effort to educe that which is found from the searching itself; and in this searching, he sought to find a firm basis, to find in it a new ground under his feet—in metaphysics. The discovery of the instability of the world around us leads Plato to see that on the basis of which the instability of things around me first opens up to me. He sees that there is no measure here. Later Plato says that the measure is real being. And this attempt to jump out of this searching onto new, firm ground, then for millennia, becomes a great model and, at the same time, a seduction.

This would mean describing the entire history of philosophy, even the whole history of human thought. This path of reflecting off from non-problematic reality; of searching, the effort to find new ground in searching itself; of problematizing that which is found; the path always again renewed; the path, in the end, leads to a certain discovery, but not to what philosophy had expected at the beginning. What philosophy

---

[5] Heraclites, Fr. B 64. *Ed.*

found in the end was not new ground to stand on, but rather only a new way of dealing with the old ground.

That which philosophy found at the beginning of the modern era we no longer call philosophy but rather science. This is the new certainty, if you like; a certainty that is the result of philosophical searching that is the result of a spiritual activity, that offers something firm, that offers the possibility of mastering our life and the world around us, but in a special way—so that this negative now becomes the basis. In science we no longer have the experience of the *problematicity* of life and the *problematicity* of reality, but rather we have the experience of the privation of any kind of meaning. What science provides – at least science as it has been conceived since the 17th century and in the direction it continues to advance ever more perfectly – is a reality truly deprived of all meaning. This is precisely why we can do whatever we want with it, and why it seems to us like a simple reservoir of forces. This is the result of a *spiritual activity*, the result of a spiritual struggle of many long centuries. But this spiritual struggle continues on, and its results have been more and more negative for a long time. Nevertheless it is a life of the spirit, it is a path on which this spiritual person must travel, which he cannot avoid: sometimes it looks as if the result of the whole adventure of the spiritual life is that we find ourselves once again at the beginning, where this whole movement started: simply in that life, which is given to us and beyond which we cannot go further.

This is the cruelest situation for the spiritual person—this final resulting suspension, this final resulting skepticism, the disappointment in the attempts at searching thus far, which again and again appear empty and futile. Confronted with this situation, the spiritual life itself is understandably not enticing. It is as if it abandons itself, as if it devalues itself. It is neither accidental nor insubstantial that, after millennia of monumental effort, philosophy is ruled by something that could be called nihilism. That all this searching is the basis upon which spiritual life today develops and comes to the conclusion that life and the world are not only problematic, but that meaning as an answer to this question is not only not found, but even that it *cannot* be found, that the final result is *nihil*: a self-negation, a self-denial.

How does it look when we confront the pretensions of the spiritual person with this situation, the pretensions that he declared from the very beginning, that he posed on the life of the community?

Socrates and Plato were problematizers of life. They were people who did not accept reality as it is presented, but rather saw it as shaken—but the consequence they derived from this shaking was preciscly that some kind of peculiar, *other* life *is possible*; there is another direction of life possible, something like a *new ground*, and only here is it possible to measure what is and what is not. They were so firmly convinced of this that they challenged this naive and banal reality in battle. We know how Plato defined the position of the spiritual person in the world and in society; one of the reasons we always read Plato's works, especially the work about the state, with such anticipation is that they contain the classically defined relationship of the spiritual person to the whole of society—to the society that was then, and many times we feel that it is also very relevant to the society that is now.

Plato says there are only three possible attitudes:

One is the path that Socrates took—to show people how things are in reality, that the world is dark, problematic, that *we do not possess it*; but this means coming *into conflict* and going to one's death. The logic of this process is rigorously enacted in Plato.

The second possibility is the one that Plato chooses—internal emigration, withdrawal from the public, withdrawal from contact and conflict with the world (and mainly with the community) in the hope that, through philosophical searching, we will find something, like a community of spiritual people, that will make it possible for spiritual people to live and not die.

And the third possibility is to become a sophist. There are no other possibilities.

You see – when we express it in this way – that there is something in this whose strength and relevance we feel still today. Of course, we do so with the assumption that we will not obtain the agreement of those who regard skepticism as the last word.

Philosophers like Socrates and Plato are not sophists, but rather they are real spiritual people searching and fighting with the greatest sincerity to prevent us from being deceived by illusions and inventing some illusory world of our own upon which we could supposedly be able to stand firmly. That they are the ones who wanted to search most radically, of that, I think, there is no doubt. This is the challenge put forth by these philosophers, of these great destroyers and great rebels who refused to give in to let themselves become drunk on any illusions, who did not want to leave this problematicity—and it is in this that they are spiritual and philosophical. This great challenge is, to the greatest degree, truly relevant.

But how is it possible that these philosophers, these spiritual people, address us at all? How is it possible that they consider it appropriate to speak to us, that they consider it possibly worthwhile? Each such address is a certain act, but each act has meaning only when it makes sense to do it, when something speaks to us, when some reality addresses us. But where nothing has any value or worth, it does not make sense to even speak. Isn't this the inconsistency in the nihilism of those who deny instead of problematizing? Is the last word of problematizing negation? Or is problematizing something fundamentally different from negation, something, in a way, more negative than mere negation. And precisely because of this, doesn't it make a certain life program possible after all? Maybe if we return to the beginning of this problematizing something will dawn on us.

We said that wherever we are struck by a strange sense of wonder about everything that surrounds us, of that in which we are, in which we act and react, there in reality no new thing is revealed to us, no new reality. Yet still *something* is revealed, which is not an absolute nothing, or which is mere nothing only from the point of view of the reality of things. Does this not suggest that there belongs to the nature of reality – if we take it as a whole, namely as a reality that reveals itself – something that is in itself problematic, that is in itself a question, that is *darkness*. This is not a darkness that is perhaps only our subjective unfamiliarity, our subjective ignorance, but rather something that is a *precondition* for something to appear in the world at all. And precisely the fact that something appears in the world, that the world appears, this is the most fundamental fact of reality—of the reality that we live, the reality that is a phenomenon.

So although at this point we do not get any firm ground of some reality, it is revealed to us that this questioning is not only a subjective caprice on our part after all, that it is not only one attitude among many other possible attitudes, that it is not something arbitrary. Rather it is something founded on the deepest basis of our life, only *here* do we stand on our own ground—not there, where we initially supposed. And perhaps precisely *here* also lies the possibility for all those who are searching, and all those who presume to have found and those who show them that they have not found, and those who delight in once again having caught a glimpse of something—precisely here is the possibility for all of these in their disagreement, to be able to agree on one fundamental level, i.e., on the level of the spiritual life.

Thus, in the spiritual life it is possible to find unity precisely *without firm ground*, and it is possible to overcome this absolute negativity, negative skepticism, negative nihilism without being dogmatic.

In one respect, the present situation of the spiritual person admittedly looks, as I attempted to show, especially radically harsh. When we see, face to face with today's most radical thinkers, that it is as if the great spiritual acts of the past have disintegrated, and as though the spiritual life itself forced us to abandon and be skeptical of them (specifically, to abandon metaphysical questioning and metaphysical solutions), it seems to prove the opponents of spiritual life right. That is why we also see that the world and life of today is in reality, and with such a clear conscience, non-spiritual. On one hand, the situation in the present era looks less hopeful and harsher than it has at any other time in history, but on the other hand, it can be said that certain moments exist that do not cast the contemporary situation in the worst light Several of which I shall mention here:

First, contemporary nihilism is itself developing in a certain way: today one can already speak of the history of contemporary nihilism. One author[6] distinguishes three phases in contemporary nihilism that, beginning with Nietzsche, gained ground as a certain thought construct. The author that I am thinking about discerns joyful, creative nihilism where an optimistic attitude is derived from the understanding that reality is completely nonsensical. Thus, it is possible to behave toward reality in whatever way we want and form it arbitrarily according to our will. This attitude – confronted with the impossibility of forming reality according to the will of anybody – changes into a nihilism of self-subordination to a particular objective power. I will not describe this in more detail, since you all know that these phenomena are exceedingly widespread; the entire history of recent decades, both world wars, and the periods between and since them are full of these phenomena.

---

[6] Cf. H. Gollwitzer – W. Weischedel, *Denken und Glauben*, Stuttgart 1965, pp. 268–274. W. Weischedel, *Der Gott der Philosophen*, Vol. 2, München 1971, pp. 165–182. *Ed.*

Second, after the Second World War, the nihilism of resignation was talked about, a nihilism that does not know what to do, which is not interested in any attitude, is absolutely unanchored, refuses every solution, and also refuses all help.

And the final version already resembles something like an inner mental paralysis. It also begins to realize that all of nihilism up to now has not been radical enough, namely, that it itself is missing skepticism towards skepticism. However, it does not have enough strength to pull itself together in this attitude that is beginning to have something positive within it. Nevertheless, this skepticism towards skepticism, this possible suspension of absolute negation, is the result of consistently thinking through this thought, but this consistent thinking through means nothing other than the path back to Ancient Socraticism.

Another special aspect in the present era (and it is no accident that it is in the present era) is the element of our spiritual life, of our historical horizon, that possibly contributes most to the universal spread of nihilistic thoughts and moods, namely science, is beginning to discover in itself a skepticism towards the nihilistic concept of science, towards that concept of science as factological without any kind of meaning. We see this even in that the most objective sciences, e.g., physics, are aware today of the limits of objectification. It is also noticeable in the penetration of structuralist tendencies, since structuralism everywhere means not only reasoning from the point of view of the whole, but also from the point of view of meaning. Structures are *meaningful* structures. Contemporary structuralism is not yet fully aware of the entire extent of this shift that by its influence is being introduced into science. This structural shift first gains its full significance in connection with yet another important phenomenon of the present. This final motif is the discovery of the openness of Man. It was precisely this discovery of the openness of Man that negated the concept of existent and Being. This concept enabled the development of modern mathematical, natural science, and consequently also of factological science and its concept of reality, which also encompasses the famous Cartesian dualism, i.e., the division of the world into subject and object. Human openness disputes the subject, disputes this duality, and enables a different view of phenomenon, of the appearance of reality and the appearance of the world as a whole.

Right now, all these phenomena are only a sort of twilight, indicating perhaps that midnight no longer rules.

One more thing comes to mind, however, which is that in effect everything in this cruel world we have experienced and are experiencing, the cruel world of two wars and terrible revolutions, of everything we see around ourselves, is not comprehensible, I think, in any other way than this: that the people who exposed themselves to these terrible catastrophes did not succumb to them only passively, but went into Moloch's jaws for the most part voluntarily, even happily ... this involved something like a certain awareness that this immediate life and world are not everything, that it is possible to sacrifice them, and that in this sacrifice it is possible to catch a glimpse of this thunderbolt in the darkness. This, I think, is what lies behind the horrors of our time.

If we have to educe some kind of sum from all of this, then maybe we could say that the spiritual person today has no reason for resignation. The spiritual person today can once again see certain possibilities. The spiritual person must cease being afraid, and the basis for him not to be afraid lies precisely in that which he is able to catch glimpse of.

The spiritual person who is capable of sacrifice, who is capable of *seeing* its significance and meaning – as I attempted to indicate – *cannot* be afraid. The spiritual person is not of course a politician and is not political in the usual sense of this word. He is not a party to the dispute that rules this world—but he is political in yet a different way, obviously, and he cannot be apolitical because this *non-self-evident nature of reality* is precisely what he throws into the face of this society and of everything that he finds around himself.

This conflict that Plato spoke about is a phenomenon. Here we return to what we were saying before about the relevance of *Politeia*. Life in this position is precisely what the positive powers of reality do not tolerate and do not want to see, what they cannot account for, and against which they fight with all their strength—it is something that they cannot endure. And here this spiritual person must, of course, advocate his position. This does not mean engaging in some kind of propaganda. I simply either avow what I indicated to be the program of the spiritual life, or not—either I am this spiritual person, or I am simply a sophist, I am merely a pretender, and this is then that usual culture and literature and the other ways that people make a living. But to pretend to be a spiritual person by saying that politics is something unworthy of one's own spiritual activity, that it destroys and frustrates the spiritual activity—this is the worst sophistry imaginable.

So these are the comments that I wanted to present to you today. I wanted to emphasize the difference between what is called culture (which is a kind of external fact – a sociological reality that is something absolutely ambiguous if we look at it from the viewpoint that there exists an attempt to live in truth) and what I called the spiritual life, which is something completely different.

Thus, this is my basic thesis, and now we can debate about it ...

Discussion

A: Is it incompatible with the program of the spiritual life if someone performs some kind of profession within the framework of a concrete society which, although it does not fulfill the aspirations of the spiritual life, does provide, however, a livelihood, which then in turn allows one opportunity to dedicate oneself to more fundamental things...?

P: Why would it be incompatible? A livelihood is a livelihood. Only one is not allowed to think that because one writes on paper one is already a spiritual person.

A: Does this then mean self-reflection ...!? As long as one is aware of this, and aware also of this skepticism that arises from this—skepticism towards one's position as an intellectual, in other words, as a sophist...

P: If I am an intellectual, I do not have to be a sophist...!

A: I had the impression that you understand intellectualism as a modern term for the Platonic concept of the sophist...

P: That is already something else ... Sophistry originates where one does not differentiate.

A: I had the impression that what Plato called sophistry is, in modern times, precisely intellectualism, because these sophists also only made their living by this and were also not convinced of it. But perhaps it is possible – as long as this sophist is aware that it is a particular trade for him – that, besides this, he could be a Socratic person as well; and that perhaps the very same situation also exists in the modern era.

P: In Plato, the sophist is a somewhat complicated problem. What is the situation with the livelihood? ... Plato really perceives a shortcoming already in the fact that these people live off of this. But this is not the substantial matter—the substantial matter is this: the sophist is possible only on the basis of the existence of the spiritual person. Sophists were possible only on the basis of the philosophers existing beforehand. The sophists saw at once that there was a wonderful possibility for making a living off of this; that it is possible to make from this an excellent thing for demagoguery, for example; that it is possible to practice rhetoric and other such tricks that wonderfully suited them for their practical needs and life. ... And suddenly by doing this they drastically narrowed the horizon of the spiritual life, they provincialized and degraded everything. That is what Plato reproached them for! They simply did not see the kind of essential human possibility they projected for what it was, so that it became so insubstantial, and just one of many possibilities.

And if I attempt to generalize from our viewpoint, as I tried to outline, that the spiritual person is he who is aware of the problematicity of the world and of life, and derives from this a life program, his life basis, possibly it could be ambiguous: Afterwards it is quite clear that this person must make a living somehow. That he makes a living one way or another is quite arbitrary. The important point is that he must be faithful to his spiritual program. If that livelihood leads him to stop being faithful to it, then it is clear that in reality he was not a spiritual person, but rather that sophist, who only pretended to be a spiritual person but was a parasite on spiritual life. And this is how it always is, over and over again; we still see this around us every day. We see these occurrences of parasites on the spiritual life, this is not a figment of our imagination, this is a phenomenon, even though at first glance they look much the same as the spiritual person in the usual empirical world: they write books and articles (today these two are relatively clearly differentiated, since there are those who write for themselves and those who write for newspapers). But in the end this abstract talk is directed towards certain concrete things in our normal life.

B: So in this attitude of the spiritual person there is, at the same time, something like a lack of respect, a disdain for the person of culture?

P: Disdain ... I think it is disdain from both sides. But this disdain is not what is substantial, since the spiritual person above all has enough work with his problems and this non-spiritual person has enough work with his career, rather than to be occupied with the sphere of disdain...

B: I meant it a little differently—not as the separation of these two subjects, but their concurrent presence: the spiritual person who is occupied with some kind of cultural activity must have inside himself a modus of a certain lack of respect for this activity in order to maintain the ability to work on his advancement as a spiritual person...

P: A lack of respect no—just the opposite. He must take this activity of his very seriously, so as not to denigrate it. He knows that if he is going to write, then it must become an expression of his spiritual life, and only that way does it have meaning and value. This is simply a given in his life program, he does not need to somehow specially concentrate on this and to contemplate about it—it is a matter-of-course for him. Therefore, also for him it is a matter-of-course that he cannot be shaken in this position, since for him that would mean to stop existing. A person who is this way truly – and in this lies the precise meaning of "truly", in this there is a piece of the personal – who truly goes in this direction, he has his path clearly before him.

A: Then this person is in such a position that he must wait for certain moments when he realizes his spiritual life in reality, when he publicly expresses it...

P: That is not quite right. Under certain circumstances one waits, under certain circumstances one creates. I think that some courageous people, even under the most horrible circumstances, are able to form reality to a certain degree. I did not explicitly mention this aspect: the spiritual life is not just meditation or the creation of artistic works, the spiritual life is precisely also action based on the insight that reality is not rigid, on recognizing plasticity of reality. There are people who see a certain situation as hopeless while assuming that they are being absolutely objective – Edvard Beneš in 1938 for example[7] – and they do not realize that where they see no way out is where in reality their greatest chance lies. This may happen. I am not saying that the spiritual life consists in banging one's head against the wall, but it is not possible to express it the way you did.

A: I wanted to talk about certain moments when...

P: One always acts only in moments—life for the most part is not composed of *real* actions; most of the time life is composed of stereotypical reactions. The kind of opportunities when one really acts, when

---

[7] In 1938, the Czechoslovak President Beneš did not realize that it was possible for him to refuse the Munich Agreement and unilaterally defend Czechoslovakia from Hilter. *Ed.*

a possibility is seen that is not banal, and when people take the possibility upon themselves with full responsibility—these opportunities are rare.

A: Thus, such biding of one's time, which justifies itself by the necessity of a situation, is also a manifestation of sophistry...

P: Plato said about himself that he must bide his time, and at the same time we know, of course, how he did this. He bid his time, this is true; he bid his time by writing *Politeia* and going to Sicily ... There were many reasons for retreating from the Athenian polis, and the most substantial one was Socrates—but this was not a retreat from spiritual politics. Plato's internal emigration is only an emigration from the Athenian polis, not from politics in general.

C: I had the impression from your lecture that the spiritual person's life consists of seeing problematicity—as if seeing problematicity was the most important sign of the spiritual life. But the great intellectual and poetical personalities of the 19th and 20th centuries, who witnessed this problematicity most acutely and therefore, in the sense of your lecture, are so keenly spiritual, at certain moments seem as though they were unable to endure or maintain this spirituality, in the sense of problematicity, and escaped to something else, to a fascination with something that is the opposite of spirituality, namely simplicity and non-problematicity. These are the yearnings for the universal rootedness of the medieval person or the rootedness of peasant life. Can the spiritual person, in this problematicity – in something that is difficult to endure – survive? And isn't the product of this such an escape?

P: This is a very essential question: we cannot understand history at all without this. An example of this is the monumental historical phenomenon of Christianity. This exactly is seeing problematicity while simultaneously trying to escape it, but this problematicity is there. This is important: it is an escape on the background of problematicity. In the end, you have this with all the Christian thinkers. St. Paul starts with this, the σοφία τοῦ κόσμου[8]: the more you strain, the more futile it is, and what Man cannot do is easy for God—therefore we must believe ... But *he knows* about this problematicity, this desire to escape is based on this. And this appears again with Pascal!

---

[8] "wisdom of the world" – See New Testament, Paul, Letters to the Corinthians, 1,20 *Ed.*

C: He not only knows about it, he even proclaims it. A problem-free religion...

P: That is impossible!

A: I remember that in one discussion I used the phrase "to rest in dogma" and a theologian who was present became upset that I imagined dogma as a tub to recline in – a person does not rest in dogma, it is something doubted and alive – it is a new turmoil ... and he was decidedly not a heretical priest...

P: Arousing the problematic belongs to the nature of Christianity. There is no doubt that Christianity first and foremost wants to rouse Man from this non-problematicity. *Memento mori*, remember the whole vale of tears. There is a harsh side of reality here. But then comes the turning point.

Now concerning these escapes: Christianity is not alone here in stressing problematicity. This is in all of metaphysics. All of metaphysics arises from this: it begins with wonder and searching. Plato was not writing about anything other than this searching itself. In all that we have preserved from Plato, nowhere is there any doctrine. And yet he had a doctrine, and what a doctrine! This was the main thing for him! And yet, the great thing in Plato is that he did not write it. *He did not write it!* That in which he believed most profoundly and towards which he was oriented—he did not write it! Sometimes he lectured it—and we have evidence of this, and a doctrine can be constructed from this (philologists have been quite successful at this). But what Plato authentically wrote, what he wanted to leave behind, is exclusively problematic and aporetic in character. Metaphysics is, of course, a searching that stops somewhere, but its fate lies in that it starts again, and the turning point, which is perhaps necessary to carry out face to face with metaphysics' catastrophes, is that it is necessary to remind metaphysics not of what it sees in the thunderbolt but rather of that *thunderbolt!* In the thunderbolt, metaphysics catches a glimpse of *something*, a glimpse of an idea, or of something like Aristotle's amazing deity, νόησις νοήσεως,[9] which is an eternal actuality. But it is possible to catch a glimpse of something only when the lightning flashes and tears through the darkness. And this darkness is precisely this

---

[9]   Aristotle, *Metaphysics*, XII, 9, 1074b34–35. *Ed.*

problematicity, which I did not invent, which is a condition for anything to appear to me at all.

There is one more thing that I would like to add to what I have improvised here.

We are all often dispirited and would like to just exhale and live, but let's look at history, which teaches us that the spiritual life has always been difficult, always under pressure and always impeded, always in conflict. This situation, as Plato depicts it, the three possibilities, this is how it always was from the time history began. Since history began with the spiritual life, history began with this awareness of problematicity. Up to that time, Man no doubt often had some kind of mysterious reality before him, but not problematicity as such.

That is the first thing. And the second is that – who knows – maybe reality is precisely in this situation of problematicity, and in this situation is our only chance to truly live. Yet reality is resistance, it is that which poses resistance to us and we, on our part, stand in its way. Life without this tonus is like nothing, it is what flows like water, what passes away.

Why exactly did I come to speak to you about this? We are all full of sadness over certain events that cause us sorrow. So a person poses the question to himself: how to speak to the people close to him and the young, how to tell them how a person who has lived through so many conflicts in his life looks upon it all... So let's go home, shall we?

The Political Philosophy
of a Non-Political Philosopher

by Eric Manton

Why would anyone want to study the political philosophy of someone who is not considered to be a political philosopher? If this philosopher also happened to be one of the founders of a human rights dissident movement, would that be enough of a justification to research his political philosophy, or "that which is political" in his thought? Is the fact that this philosopher influenced generations of dissidents who later became politicians and was the teacher of most of the main philosophers in Prague reason enough to seek to understand his observations on the nature of politics? Is the fact that this philosopher, who was the most important Czech philosopher of the 20th century, also lived through two world wars, one invasion, and two occupations, grew up and reached adulthood in a democratic "island", and then spent almost thirty years of his life under a repressive totalitarian regime, sufficient explanation for wanting to understand his reflection on the political? All of these factors point to the value of focusing upon the political aspects of Jan Patočka's thought. The dramatic dissident end of Patočka's life already makes studying this aspect of his philosophy worthwhile. However, when looking closer, one realizes that his dissident activities were not only a reaction to the political situations of the time, but rather were rooted in the core of his philosophy.

In the English literature on Patočka's philosophy, examinations of his reflections on the political have mainly been made in connection with his last great work, the *Heretical Essays,* and his influence on Vaclav Hável and the Czechoslovak human rights dissident movement, Charter 77. This is an accurate approach, since Patočka's philosophy did influence greatly the Charter and its members. One could say that any study of Czech dissident political philosophy, of Czech philosophy of dissidence, must have Patočka at its core.

However, the political engagement at the end of his life is generally considered to be an anomaly of his personal style and behavior. Yet, a closer investigation into Patočka's philosophy points to a different conclusion. Right from the beginning of his philosophical "career" he wrote about the political events that he was living through. Of course, his analysis of the historical events happening around him was not done in the style of typical contemporary political science. Patočka discussed different political programs, the nature of society, historical events, and the role of political opposition in authoritarian systems. But when writing about these subjects, he focused on a level much more fundamental than what is usually considered political science: Patočka analyzed these political topics *philosophically*. He concentrated on understanding the political from the ontological and phenomenological perspectives, looking at the historicity of human beings and the problematicity of Being, examining the existential angle on the role of the individual in society and human freedom, and he made ethical observations about the responsible manner of being for the authentic person who has little choice but to be some sort of dissident.

To truly understand the significance of this combination, it is necessary to recall a different, original concept of political philosophy rather than what prevails in the academic world today. Patočka agreed with the classic concept of political philosophy in which the soul correlates with society. Patočka talked about how Plato dealt with the issue of the soul on three levels: the ontological, the political, and the existential. "So then there are *three* currents of the care for the soul:the first is the ontological, the second is *the care for the soul in the community as the conflict of two ways of life…* and the third is *the care for the soul in the aspect of its inner life*."[1] All three levels and precisely their interconnection is the political.

Already from his earliest writings, Patočka presents his understanding of politics as concerning the historical person living philosophically within the world. Hence he focused from the beginning on an interpretation of politics that encompassed the classical multi-level, holistic view of that which is political.

---

[1] J. Patočka, *Platón a Evropa* (Plato and Europe), in: *Péče o duši 4*, Praha (Archivní soubor) 1979, p. 116.

A brief overview of the political significant aspects of Jan Patočka's personal history would be useful here. In 1932 and 1933, he studied with a Humboldt scholarship in Berlin during the rise of National Socialism and in Freiburg (where he went to study with Husserl) when Martin Heidegger was Rector. He wrote one of his first published works, "Platonism and Politics" in 1933, in which he stresses the importance of engaging in the spiritual work that is philosophy, which is "the most important and most intensive *praxis*". He critiques humanism and socialism (which he calls collectivism here) as false myths that are anti-spiritual in nature. Instead he promotes a philosophical engagement in and with society: "The philosopher as such is undoubtedly not engaged in daily political conflict, in daily *praxis*, which is always based on sophistry or mysticism, but his activity in the world is based on the philosopher possessing a political idea, on the philosopher living within Plato's political idea."

In 1934, Patočka helped found and was the Secretary of the Cercle philosophique de Prague – Prague Philosophical Circle, whose purpose was to increase the democratic understanding between Czechs and Germans, and which later became a refuge for philosophers fleeing from the academic and political repression of the ideologies ruling in the Communist Soviet Union and the Fascist Germany. "Some Comments on the Extramundane and Mundane Position of Philosophy" was published the same year. In this prophetic article, Patočka describes the relationship between philosophy and the mundane world, how because the world does not understand the philosopher, "the world" turns on the philosopher with hatred and wants to eliminate him. However, the philosopher has no choice; philosophizing is what he does, it makes him what he is; it gives him the possibility not only to seem to be, but truly to be. Here Patočka portrays Socrates as the model and his fate is inevitable for all true philosophers. Philosophy is seen as a threat, because philosophy challenges the ideologies' myths and dispels the illusions that society is led and comforted by. The philosopher problematizes and is necessarily oppressed for doing so, since he is seen as a useless trouble-maker. "The reason why philosophy actually *must be* persecuted as soon as it crystallizes in its pure form is ... that the mundane projection of philosophy appears as a decline of life." However, the Socratic philosopher cannot do otherwise, because he has "an awareness that what I do is *for me* what I must do; the sole possible manner of my being in the world." And in living according to this manner of being, the person is free. "Thus the comprehension of being, which philosophy arrives at when intellectually surpassing the world, is possible only with the genuine human being as represented by a free act. So we might, perhaps, express the ideal of a sovereign philosophy as that of a philosophy of heroism and a heroism of philosophy."

During the period leading up to the Second World War, Patočka wrote in favor of a revival of Masarykian humanism to defend the spiritual life of the country against the hostile ideologies that were looming on its borders. He tried to rally the intelligentsia to support the country in its time of spiritual and intellectual impending need. After the capitulation of the Munich Agreement, in "Reflection on Defeat", Patočka chastises this same intelligentsia, these sophists, for failing in their duty and letting their country down. He fiercely attacks the intelligentsia for being conceited, irresponsible, and uncreative. The ideals did not fail, but the people who were supposedly acting in their name failed to realize them. The sophistic intelligentsia did not act responsibly, "they do not have a vivid feeling of responsibility towards people, and the freedom that they use is not freedom of thought, because creative thought is foreign to them."

After Czechoslovakia was occupied by Nazi Germany, Patočka published "Life in Balance, Life in Amplitude". This article presented a stinging critique of the political theories that he categorized as aiming for a life in balance, into which he grouped all three theories that were soon to fight against each other—the offshoots of Enlightenment humanist ideology of Nazism, Communism, and Liberalism. He described this attitude of balance as conceiving of the person as essentially harmonious and balanced. Human nature and the process of history are fundamentally aimed toward the realization of this innate state. All human activity has harmony, balance, and happiness as its orientation. Human beings may be incomplete and imperfect, but this will be remedied by the appropriate measures of education and social organization. Patočka criticizes this attitude for its closed concept of Man, its tendency to resist and suppress (even violently) anything that is not "normal," to ignore or discount anything that shakes this balanced picture of life, and to see society as basically a technical problem that can be solved through rationality or a necessary historical development. He attacks this attitude for its deterministic approach to the concept of Man and all social activity. He says that the life in balance sees Man as "a finite, closed creature enclosed in a firm form of life, and thus history is a finished process, searching for balance is justified as striving for the aim of human society and all of the failures of our social efforts are only imperfections which will finally someday come to fruition." Patočka exposes the fact that reality corresponds so little to this fundamental ideology and suggests that a more accurate description would be a life in amplitude, in which Man can never be closed into a definitive form and where he is most human when living in problematicity. Once again, Patočka warns of the dangers of the predominant political theories of "the world" of the time and how they will oppress whoever challenges their view by questioning them. The people who live in amplitude "protest vigorously against the all too human illusions, against the naive paradises of the huddled, 'harmonic' souls, against those life dreams in the calm, untroubled tracks of employment, work, usual obligations, utility, harmony, and happiness. They also look for their paradise, but it is not a paradise of closed, but rather open eyes."

After the Second World War and the return of a liberal democracy, Patočka started working at Charles University. In 1946, he wrote "Ideology and Life in the Idea", which critiques the ideologies that had just fought each other in the war, including the one that was gaining power in Czechoslovakia at the time, socialist humanism manifesting as Communism. He analyzed socialism as multifaceted in that, at the same time, it appeals to Man spiritually, it objectifies Man, and it controls Man for external social aims through ideology. Patočka critiques socialism, which would soon take over his country, for treating people merely as material that can be manipulated by the state because it leaves out the Idea of Man—human freedom. Unfortunately, for Patočka and the rest of Czechoslovakia, his analysis was an accurate prediction.

After the Communists took power in 1948, Patočka was dismissed from the two universities he was teaching at because he refused to join the Communist Party. He would not teach at Charles University again for twenty years. Patočka was given the opportunity to join the party and continue teaching, but he decided not to. Instead, in the much more constricted circumstances with less options, he still found a way to continue with his philosophical work by focusing on Masaryk and Comenius. Unfortunately, this meant not having official direct contact with students. Even though he was given the chance to continue teaching, he refused and did not collaborate.

When he was able to return to teaching without collaborating during the thaw of the Prague Spring, he returned to the universities and was even named a Professor. He wrote about the situation around him with some optimism and hoped for the realization of the possibility that a new spiritual authority in a "mass technical intelligentsia" whose model would be the heretic that would fulfill the Socratic philosophical role previously promoted, "The task of the intelligentsia is ... on the basis of uncovering the inadequacies of the factual world, to strive for a real rule of the spirit."[2]

This historical window proved to be very brief since the new freedoms were suppressed by the invasion of the Warsaw Pact troops and the subsequent period of "Normalization". Once again, Patočka was seen as a threat and was dismissed from the universities in 1973–this time under the guise of early retirement. However, Patočka did not stop teaching; he continued by giving the so-called "apartment seminars", which included "Plato and Europe" and the "Heretical Essays". In 1973, Patočka, without permission and illegally, traveled to the 15th Philosophical Congress in Varna, Bulgaria, where he went to inform the wider philosophical community about the true, brutal conditions of engaging in philosophy under Normalization. He was prevented from finishing his speech and upon returning home was forbidden from ever traveling out of the country again. Once again, Patočka, fulfilling his philosophical duty, was seen as a threat by the state, which reacted with even stronger repressive measures against him.

During these dark days of Normalization, in which the state tried in many ways to break the free will that society had expressed during the Prague Spring and to force as many people as possible to collaborate, Patočka gave a seminar in 1975 called "The Spiritual Person and the Intellectual". The purpose of this lecture was to explain to his young students, who were suffering from the recent events, "how a person who has lived through so many conflicts in his life looks upon it all". In explaining the difference between the spiritual person and the intellectual – between the contemporary versions of the philosopher and the sophist – Patočka reaffirms the importance of living philosophically, especially in times of collaboration and oppression. For his

---

2 "Inteligence a opozice" (The Intelligentsia and Opposition), in: *O smysl dneška*, Purley (Rozmluvy) 1987, p. 18.

students, he sought to show that, even amidst harsh circumstances, a person who continues to question, continues to live in problematicity, can find a new life of freedom. He again puts Socrates forward as the role model of the constant searching and problematizing as the proper approach within the world. This manner of being is necessarily political: "The spiritual person is not, of course, a politician and is not political in the usual sense of this word. He is not a party to the dispute that rules this world—but he is political in yet a different way, obviously, and he cannot be apolitical because this *non-self-evident nature of reality* is precisely what he throws into the face of this society and of everything that he finds around himself." He warns of the predictable consequences of living this way in that the "normal" society will react against his spiritual person. "Life in this position is precisely what the positive powers of reality do not tolerate and do not want to see, what they cannot account for, and against which they fight with all their strength—it is something that they cannot endure." Patočka considers the spiritual life, lived free through sacrifice and the recognition of problematicity, also consists of action, which is taken when a possibility appears that is not banal; a possibility for the person to act with full responsibility.

In his various works spanning his entire life, Patočka used many terms to try to describe his comprehension of this political and existential aspect: Plato's political concept, transcendence, a calling or mission, human freedom, life as possibilities, titanism, a life lived out of freedom, "the strength of self-being in faithlessness", history as a creative impulse, cultivation, life in amplitude, life in the Idea, problematicity, negativity, *polemos*, the care for the soul. All of these ideas are concerned with the nature of the individual, finite, historical human being and attempt to describe different aspects of the authentic manner of being within the world.

Patočka states that the proper manner of being, the authentic way of life, is engaging in philosophy, striving to become a philosopher, and living philosophically. This manner of being is situated within the world—a world that continuously seeks to imposed itself and to constrict us with ideology and with its closed concept of Man. Since the philosopher recognizes the problematicity in Being itself, he also recognizes the problematicity in the constructs and programs of the world. This recognition of problematicity allows the philosopher an opportunity to grasp his freedom in spite of the oppressing "world".

The philosopher, for Patočka, is the person who seeks to cultivate his soul, to learn about that which is, to understand the whole. He is a person who is willing and unafraid of sacrifice because he understands its meaning and significance. He is continuously living in negativity and problematicity, which necessarily put him at odds with society "into whose face he throws" their shortcomings. Yet the philosopher is also someone on a mission, who feels responsible for his actions in the world as well as responsibility to spread and foster this awareness, this awakening, in others like himself.

In 1975, Patocka still has hope in the technical intelligentsia, which has transformed now into the "solidarity of the shaken" as the spiritual authority. The solidarity of the shaken is a group of people banded together to resist what in the *Heretical Essays* he called Force, they are those who understand, those who know the significance of sacrifice, and are willing to risk their lives. This group of spiritual people retains the Socratic, philosophical elements of the shaking, the living in problematicity, the constant questioning, the confronting of society with the inadequacies and the non-obviousness of reality. "The solidarity of the shaken can say 'no'… It will not offer positive programs but will speak, like Socrates' *daimonion*, in warnings and prohibitions."[3]

About one year after *The Heretical Essays*, he encountered a scattered, eclectic group of artists, punk rockers, playwrights, theologians, and former communists. In this group of spiritual people, he found what he had been looking for so long, a movement of philosophers, those who lived for others, who were the center of the morality of the social whole, who were "the role models for everybody else". He discovered Charter 77. And even though he was reluctant to take an active role, for he always considered his personal spiritual activity to consist in teaching, he became one of its representatives, one of its leaders. Patočka perceived Charter 77 in terms of this Socratic political movement. He emphasized that Charter 77 was not a typical political act, it was not an organization nor an association, but rather based on individuals upholding their sense of duty, their "obligation to speak out for himself—which is his obligation to his society as well."[4] Thus Charter

---

[3] J. Patočka, *Heretical Essays in the Philosophy of History* (Kacířské eseje o filosofii dějin), Chicago (Open Court) 1996, p. 135.

[4] J. Patočka, "The Obligation to Resist Injustice" (Čím je a čím není Charta

77 was a movement in the philosophical sense since its role was to point out the inadequacies in society, to expose society and the forces of the Day to problematicity, and to make the members of society aware of their rights as humans, "for what speaks here is nothing but a respect for humans and for the common good that makes us human, a respect present in every individual."[5] The task of Charter 77 was to *shake* "the confidence of the mighty" and bear testimony to injustice. For Patočka, this was truly a philosophical movement, a movement by which we learn and form ourselves:

> "The Charter never sought more than to educate. But what does this mean? Every person must learn for himself, though often he can be affected by examples, warned by bad results, or taught by conversation and discussion. Education means coming to understand that there is more to life than fear and gain ... It is the hope of Charta 77 that our citizens may learn to act as free persons, self-motivated and responsible."[6]

Thus, Charter 77 became the realization of Patočka's philosophical problematic heroes, those which he had spent his whole life trying to discover, explain, inspire, and cultivate. In the end, he became one of their leaders and eventually, after his ultimate sacrifice, its symbol. It was a sacrifice, and Patočka, being one who understood the meaning and significance of sacrifice, was aware of this. Forty years earlier, Patočka called for a philosophy of heroism and a heroism of philosophy, and by living his life through philosophy, that authentic manner of being, he heeded that challenge himself and became a hero. Patočka also became a role model of the morality for the social whole and his influence on Czech society is still felt up to the present day. Through his example and the example for those he taught and inspired, "our people have once more become aware that there are things for which it

---

77), in: *Jan Patočka: Philosophy and Selected Writings*, E. Kohák (ed.), Chicago (University of Chicago Press) 1989, p. 342.

[5] Ibid.

[6] J. Patočka, "What We Can and Cannot Expect from Charta 77" (Co můžeme očekávat od Charty 77?), in: *Jan Patočka: Philosophy and Selected Writings*, E. Kohák (ed.), Chicago (University of Chicago Press) 1989, p. 346.

is worthwhile to suffer, that the things for which we might have to suffer are those which make life worthwhile..."[7]

Patočka developed a political philosophy essentially corresponding to the model of Socrates. Socrates probably did not consider himself to be especially "political" in the modern sense of the term. He was just living his life as he felt and knew that he had to. Of course, this consisted of constant questioning and throwing problematicity into the face of the polis. As Patočka wrote in 1934, society, the state, "the world" turned against Socrates with hatred because he was seen as a threat to their comforting illusions and to their systems of manipulating and controlling Man. Socrates did not choose to be a dissident – the polis interpreted his manner of being as a threat and made him a dissident. Likewise, Patočka did his duty of caring for his soul and "for the soul in the community" by teaching, as that was his responsibility. When he found himself in the historical circumstances out of which the Charter arose, he was asked to slightly alter his mode of engagement. He would still teach through writing and talking to people, but just on a larger scale. He seized this possibility and with it his freedom, and he accepted the responsibility for this freedom and assumed his position as drafter of the documents and spokesman of Charter 77. The reaction of the state, of "the world", was as it always has been when truth and problematicity are thrown in its face, dispelling its illusions and lies. The oppressive world of ideology, of balance, eliminated this philosopher, who lived in amplitude, who strived for the Idea of Man and human freedom, this spiritual person who lived in problematicity.

On March 13, 1977, Jan Patočka died after interrogations by police in connection with his dissident activities. He was almost 70 years old.

> "Not that Socrates' trial was something tragic for Socrates – Socrates was a 70 year-old person when he had to part with life – but the tragedy was for the community itself, since it shows its blindness, its inability to see its own role and to see what the community can be and should be."[8]

---

[7] Ibid.

[8] J. Patočka, *Platón a Evropa* (Plato and Europe), in: *Péče o duši 4*, Praha (Archvní soubor) 1979, p. 131.

Recommended Further Reading

The articles in this booklet are just a selection of texts that could be categorized as dealing with the political side of Patočka's philosophy. These particular texts were chosen to illustrate his ideas from the beginning to the end of his philosophical career, from one of his first published articles (1933) to a seminar held in the last years of his life (1975). They were also selected for their philosophical significance in that they highlight especially well Patočka's examination of the role of philosophy and the philosopher in the world, as well as the interaction between the philosopher and the world.

However, these selected articles are not the only examples of Patočka addressing these topics directly. The texts presented here are just a representative sample and for a more comprehensive understanding of Patočka's views on these topics, one can turn to a number of other texts. Erazim Kohák translated some of these in his important book that provided an introduction to Patočka for the English-speaking world, *Jan Patočka: Philosophy and Selected Writings*, Chicago (University of Chicago Press) 1989.

1936: "Masaryk's and Husserl's Conception of the Spiritual Crisis of Europe" (Masarykovo a Husserlovo pojetí duševní krise evropského lidstva), pp. 145–156.
1936: "Titanism" (Titanismus), pp. 139–144.
1953: "Negative Platonism" (Negativní platonismus), pp. 175–206.
1977: "The Obligation to Resist Injustice" (Čím je a čím není Charta 77), pp. 340–343.
1977: "What We Can and Cannot Expect from Charta 77" (Co můžeme očekávat od Charty 77?), pp. 340–343.

Kohák also translated Patočka's main later work, which is also significant for discerning that which is political in his thought, the 1975 *Heretical Essays in the Philosophy of History* (Kacířské eseje o filosofii dějin), Chicago (Open Court) 1996.

Another important work that truly illustrates the Platonic influence on Patočka's thought about the Socratic position of the philosopher in the world is *Plato and Europe*, Stanford (Stanford University Press) 2002, translated by Petr Lom.

Other works by Patočka that are worth being considered for any study of Patočka's political philosophy, and are not yet translated into English (though many are in German and French), would include:

Platonism and Popularization (Platon a popularizace) – 1934

Some Comments Concerning the Concepts of History and Historiography (Několik poznámek k pojmům dějin a dějepisu) – 1934

Some Comments Concerning the Concept of World History (Několik poznámek o pojmu světových dějin) – 1935

On Two Conceptions of the Meaning of Philosophy (O dvojím pojetí smyslu filosofie) – 1936

The Idea of Liberal Education and its Contemporary Relevance (Myšlenka vzdělanosti a její aktuálnost) – 1938

The Harmonism of Modern Humanists (Harmonismus moderních humanistů) – 1939

Philosophy in the Present Situation (Filosofie v dnešní situace) – 1939

Philosophy of History (Filosofie dějin) – 1940

European Reason (Evropský rozum) – 1941

World View, World Image, Philosophy (Světový názor, obraz světa, filosofie) – 1942

Notes on Ancient Humanity. Struggle and Peace (Poznámky o antické humanitě. Boj a smír – 1945–1946

Super-Civilization and its Internal Conflict (Nadcivilizace a její vnitrní konflikt) – 1950's

Europe and the Post-European Era (Evropa a doba poevropská) – late 1960's, unfinished manuscript originally in German

The Intelligentsia and Opposition (Inteligence a opozice) – 1969

Our National Program and Today (Náš národní program a dnešek) – 1969

The Spiritual Bases of Our Time (Duchovní základy života v naší době) – 1970

The Technical *Epoché* and Sacrifice (Technická epocha a oběť) – 1973

On Masaryk's Philosophy of Religion (Kolem Masarykovy filosofie náboženství) – 1975–1976

The Heroes of Our Time (Hrdinové naší doby) – 1977

Bibliographical Note

The translated articles were originally published in the following and can now be found in the collected works:

Platonism and Politics
"Platonismus a politika", in: *Česká mysl* 29 (1933), n. 3–4, pp. 236–238.

Some Comments Concerning the Extramundane and Mundane Position of Philosophy
"Několik poznámek o mimosvětské a světské pozici filosofie", in: *Kvart* 2 (1934), n. 3, pp. 3–10. The translation appearing in this volume is a modified version of an unpublished translation done by Erazim Kohák, used with his generous permission.

Reflection on Defeat
"Úvaha o porážce", in: *Kritický měsíčník* 1 (1938), n. 8, pp. 380 n.

Life in Balance, Life in Amplitude
"Životní rovnováha a životní amplituda", in: *Kritický měsíčník* 2 (1939), n. 3, pp. 101–106.

Ideology and Life in the Idea
"Ideologie a život v ideji", in: *Kritický měsíčník* 7 (1946), n. 1–2, pp. 8–14

The Spiritual Person and the Intellectual
"Duchovní člověk a intelektuál", Transcript of a tape recording of the private seminar given on 11 April 1975. Originally published in samizdat by I. Chvatík, Prague 1988.

JAN PATOČKA
Living in Problematicity

Published by the Institute of Philosophy AS CR in cooperation
with OIKOYMENH society as its 606th publication. Edited
and translated by Eric Manton. Technical editor Vladimír
Nedvídek. Cover desing Zdeněk Ziegler. Typesetting
martin.tresnak@gmail.com. Printed by
Akcent Vimperk. New edition, Prague 2020,
first edition Prague 2007.
International distribution in cooperation
with Karolinum Press.

Vydal Filosofický ústav AV ČR, v. v. i.,
ve spolupráci se spolkem OIKOYMENH jako jeho
606. publikaci. Uspořádal a přeložil Eric Manton. Technická
redakce Vladimír Nedvídek. Obálku navrhl Zdeněk Ziegler.
Sazba martin.tresnak@gmail.com. Tisk Akcent Vimperk.
Nové vydání, Praha 2020, první vydání Praha 2007.